CIDER WITH ROSIE

Laurie Lee, the youngest but one of a family of eight, was born in a small unvisited Cotswold valley and lived there until he was twenty. The village in which he grew up was poor, self-sufficient, and still mainly feudal. In this account of his early years he tells of thin winters, fat summers, local legends and ghosts, of neighbours and relations, and of boys growing up against a half-pagan landscape in which violence and madness, country follies and feasts, were all part of one pastoral messpot.

Cider With Rosie

LAURIE LEE

CEDRIC CHIVERS
PORTWAY
BATH

First published 1959
by
The Hogarth Press Ltd
This Large Print edition published by
Cedric Chivers Ltd
by arrangement with the copyright holder
at the request of
The London & Home Counties Branch
of
The Library Association
1977

ISBN 0 85997 265 8

B
LEE.

Photoset and printed in Great Britain by
Redwood Burn Ltd, Trowbridge & Esher
Bound by Cedric Chivers Ltd, Bath

To my brothers and sisters
  —the half and the whole

CONTENTS

NOTE

Some parts of this book were originally published in *Orion, Encounter, The Queen* and *The Cornhill*, and two other fragments have been adapted from pieces first written for *Leader Magazine* and *The Geographical Magazine*. The book is a recollection of early boyhood, and some of the facts may be distorted by time.

CIDER WITH ROSIE

FIRST LIGHT

I WAS set down from the carrier's cart at the age of three; and there with a sense of bewilderment and terror my life in the village began.

The June grass, amongst which I stood, was taller than I was, and I wept. I had never been so close to grass before. It towered above me and all around me, each blade tattooed with tiger-skins of sunlight. It was knife-edged, dark and a wicked green, thick as a forest and alive with grasshoppers that chirped and chattered and leapt through the air like monkeys.

I was lost and didn't know where to move. A tropic heat oozed up from the ground, rank with sharp odours of roots and nettles. Snow-clouds of elder-blossom banked in the sky, showering upon me the fumes and flakes of their sweet and giddy suffocation. High overhead ran frenzied larks, screaming, as though the sky were tearing apart.

For the first time in my life I was out of the sight of humans. For the first time in my life I was alone in a world whose behaviour I could neither predict nor fathom: a world of birds that squealed, of plants that stank, of insects that sprang about without warning. I was lost and I did not expect to be found again. I put back my head and howled, and the sun hit me smartly on the face, like a bully.

From this daylight nightmare I was wakened, as from many another, by the appearance of my sisters. They came scrambling and calling up the steep rough bank, and parting the long grass found me. Faces of rose, familiar, living; huge shining faces hung up like shields between me and the sky; faces with grins and white teeth (some broken) to be conjured up like genii with a howl, brushing off terror with their broad scoldings and affection. They leaned over me—one, two, three—their mouths smeared with red currants and their hands dripping with juice.

'There, there, it's all right, don't you wail any more. Come down 'ome and we'll stuff you with currants.'

And Marjorie, the eldest, lifted me into her long brown hair, and ran me jogging down the path and through the steep rose-filled garden, and set me down on the cottage doorstep, which was our home, though I couldn't believe it.

That was the day we came to the village, in the summer of the last year of the First World

War. To a cottage that stood in a half-acre of garden on a steep bank above a lake; a cottage with three floors and a cellar and a treasure in the walls, with a pump and apple trees, syringa and strawberries, rooks in the chimneys, frogs in the cellar, mushrooms on the ceiling, and all for three and sixpence a week.

I don't know where I lived before then. My life began on the carrier's cart which brought me up the long slow hills to the village, and dumped me in the high grass, and lost me. I had ridden wrapped up in a Union Jack to protect me from the sun, and when I rolled out of it, and stood piping loud among the buzzing jungle of that summer bank, then, I feel, was I born. And to all the rest of us, the whole family of eight, it was the beginning of a life.

But on that first day we were all lost. Chaos was come in cartloads of furniture, and I crawled the kitchen floor through forests of upturned chairlegs and crystal fields of glass. We were washed up in a new land, and began to spread out searching its springs and treasures. The sisters spent the light of that first day stripping the fruit bushes in the garden. The currants were at their prime, clusters of red, black and yellow berries all tangled up with wild roses. Here was bounty the girls had

3

never known before, and they darted squawking from bush to bush, clawing the fruit like
sparrows.

Our Mother too was distracted from duty,
seduced by the rich wilderness of the garden
so long abandoned. All day she trotted to and
fro, flushed and garrulous, pouring flowers
into every pot and jug she could find on the
kitchen floor. Flowers from the garden, daisies from the bank, cow-parsley, grasses, ferns
and leaves—they flowed in armfuls through
the cottage door until its dim interior seemed
entirely possessed by the world outside—a
still green pool flooding with honeyed tides of
summer.

I sat on the floor on a raft of muddles and
gazed through the green window which was
full of the rising garden. I saw the long black
stockings of the girls, gaping with white flesh,
kicking among the currant bushes. Every so
often one of them would dart into the kitchen,
cram my great mouth with handfuls of
squashed berries, and run out again. And the
more I got, the more I called for more. It was
like feeding a fat young cuckoo.

The long day crowed and chirped and rang.
Nobody did any work, and there was nothing
to eat save berries and bread. I crawled about
among the ornaments on the unfamiliar

floor—the glass fishes, china dogs, shepherds and shepherdesses, bronze horsemen, stopped clocks, barometers and photographs of bearded men. I called on them each in turn, for they were the shrines and faces of a half-remembered landscape. But as I watched the sun move around the walls, drawing rainbows from the cut-glass jars in the corner, I longed for a return of order.

Then, suddenly, the day was at an end, and the house was furnished. Each stick and cup and picture was nailed immovably in place; the beds were sheeted, the windows curtained, the straw mats laid, and the house was home. I don't remember seeing it happen, but suddenly the inexorable tradition of the house, with its smell, chaos and complete logic, occurred as though it had never been otherwise. The furnishing and founding of the house came like the nightfall of that first day. From that uneasy loneliness of objects strewn on the kitchen floor, everything flew to its place and was never again questioned.

And from that day we grew up. The domestic arrangement of the house was shaken many times, like a snowstorm toy, so that beds and chairs and ornaments swirled from room to room, pursued by the gusty energies of Mother and the girls. But always these things resettled within the pattern of the walls, nothing escaped or changed, and so it remained for twenty years.

★   ★   ★

Now I measured that first growing year by the widening fields that became visible to me, the new tricks of dressing and getting about with which I became gradually endowed. I could open the kitchen door by screwing myself into a ball and leaping and banging the latch with my fist. I could climb into the high bed by using the ironwork as a ladder. I could whistle, but I couldn't lace my shoes. Life became a series of experiments which brought grief or the rewards of accomplishment: a pondering of patterns and mysteries in the house, while time hung golden and suspended, and one's body, from leaping and climbing, took on the rigid insanity of an insect, petrified as it were for hours together, breathing and watching. Watching the grains of dust fall in the sunny room, following an ant from its cradle to the grave, going over the knots in the bedroom ceiling—knots that ran like negroes in the dusk of dawn, or moved stealthily from board to board, but which settled again in the wax light of day no more monstrous than fossils in coal.

These knots on the bedroom ceiling were the whole range of a world, and over them my eyes went endlessly voyaging in that long primeval light of waking to which a child is condemned. They were archipelagos in a sea of blood-coloured varnish, they were armies grouped and united against me, they were the alphabet of a macabre tongue, the first book I ever learned to read.

Radiating from that house, with its crumbling walls, its thumps and shadows, its fancied foxes under the floor, I moved along paths that lengthened inch by inch with my mounting strength of days. From stone to stone in the trackless yard I sent forth my acorn shell of senses, moving through unfathomable oceans like a South Sea savage island-hopping across the Pacific. Antennae of eyes and nose and grubbing fingers captured a new tuft of grass, a fern, a slug, the skull of a bird, a grotto of bright snails. Through the long summer ages of those first few days I enlarged my world and mapped it in my mind, its secure havens, its dust-deserts and puddles, its peaks of dirt and flag-flying bushes. Returning too, dry-throated, over and over again, to its several well-prodded horrors: the bird's gaping bones in its cage of old sticks; the black flies in the corner, slimy dead; dry rags of snakes; and the crowded, rotting, silent-roaring city of a cat's grub-captured carcass.

Once seen, these relics passed within the frontiers of the known lands, to be remembered with a buzzing in the ears, to be revisited when the stomach was strong. They were the first tangible victims of that destroying force whose job I knew went on both night and day, though I could never catch him at it. Nevertheless I was grateful for them. Though they haunted my eyes and stuck in my dreams, they reduced for me the first infinite possibilities of horror. They chastened the imagination with the proof of a limited frightfulness.

From the harbour mouth of the scullery door I learned the rocks and reefs and the channels where safety lay. I discovered the physical pyramid of the cottage, its stores and labyrinths, its centres of magic, and of the green, sprouting island-garden upon which it stood. My Mother and sisters sailed past me like galleons in their busy dresses, and I learned the smells and sounds which followed in their wakes, the surge of breath, air of carbolic, song and grumble, and smashing of crockery.

How magnificent they appeared, full-rigged, those towering girls, with their flying hair and billowing blouses, their white-mast arms stripped for work or washing. At any moment one was boarded by them, bussed and buttoned, or swung up high like a wriggling fish to be hooked and held in their lacy linen.

The scullery was a mine of all the minerals of living. Here I discovered water—a very different element from the green crawling scum that stank in the garden tub. You could pump it in pure blue gulps out of the ground, you could swing on the pump handle and it came out sparkling like liquid sky. And it broke and ran and shone on the tiled floor, or quivered in a jug, or weighted your clothes with cold. You could drink it, draw with it, froth it with soap, swim beetles across it, or fly it in bubbles in the air. You could put your head in it, and open your eyes, and see the sides of the bucket buckle, and hear your caught breath roar, and work your mouth like a fish, and smell the lime from the ground. Substance of magic—which you could tear or wear, confine or scatter, or send down holes, but never burn or break or destroy.

The scullery was water, where the old pump stood. And it had everything else that was related to water: thick steam of Mondays edgy with starch; soapsuds boiling, bellying and popping, creaking and whispering, rainbowed with light and winking with a million windows. Bubble bubble, toil and grumble, rinsing and slapping of sheets and shirts, and panting Mother rowing her red arms like oars in the steaming waves. Then the linen came up on a stick out of the pot, like pastry, or woven suds, or sheets of moulded snow.

Here, too, was the scrubbing of floors and boots, of arms and necks, of red and white vegetables. Walk in to the morning disorder of this room and all the garden was laid out dripping on the table. Chopped carrots like copper pennies, radishes and chives, potatoes dipped and stripped clean from their coats of mud, the snapping of tight pea-pods, long shells of green pearls, and the tearing of glutinous beans from their nests of wool.

Grown stealthy, marauding among these preparations, one nibbled one's way like a rat through roots and leaves. Peas rolled under the tongue, fresh cold, like solid water; teeth chewed green peel of apples, acid sharp, and the sweet white starch of swedes. Beaten away by wet hands gloved with flour, one returned in a morose and speechless lust. Slivers of raw pastry, moulded, warm, went down in the shapes of men and women—heads and arms of unsalted flesh seasoned with nothing but a dream of cannibalism.

Large meals were prepared in this room, cauldrons of stew for the insatiate hunger of eight. Stews of all that grew on these rich banks, flavoured with sage, coloured with Oxo and laced with a few bones of lamb. There was, it is true, little meat at those times; sometimes a pound of bare ribs for boiling, or an occasional rabbit dumped at the door by a neighbour. But there was green food of great weight in season, and lentils and bread for ballast. Eight to ten loaves came to the house every day, and they never grew dry. We tore them to pieces with their crusts still warm, and their monotony was brightened by the objects we found in them—string, nails, paper, and once a mouse; for those were days of happy-go-lucky baking. The lentils were cooked in a great pot which also heated the water for the Saturday night baths. Our small wood-fire could heat sufficient water to fill one bath only, and this we shared in turn. Being the youngest but one, my water was always the dirtiest but one, and the implications of this privilege remain with me to this day.

⋆　　⋆　　⋆

11

Waking one morning in the white-washed bedroom, I opened my eyes and found them blind. Though I stretched them and stared where the room should be, nothing was visible but a glare of gold, flat on my throbbing eyelids. I groped for my body and found it there. I heard the singing of birds. Yet there was nothing at all to be seen of the world save this quivering yellow light. Was I dead, I wondered? Was I in heaven? Whatever it was I hated it. I had wakened too soon from a dream of crocodiles and I was not ready for this further outrage. Then I heard the girls' steps on the stairs.

'Our Marge!' I shouted, 'I can't see nothing!' And I began to give out my howl.

A slap of bare feet slithered across the floor, and I heard sister Marjorie's giggle.

'Just look at him,' she said. 'Pop and fetch a flannel, Doth—'is eyes've got stuck down again.'

The cold edge of the flannel passed over my face showered me with water, and I was back in the world. Bed and beams, and the sun-square window, and the girls bending over me grinning.

''Oo did it?' I yelled.

'Nobody, silly. Your eyes got bunged up,

that's all.'

The sweet glue of sleep; it had happened before, but somehow I always forgot. So I threatened the girls I'd bung theirs up too: I was awake, I could see, I was happy. I lay looking out of the small green window. The world outside was crimson and on fire. I had never seen it looking like that before.

'Doth?' I said, 'what's happening to them trees?'

Dorothy was dressing. She leaned out of the window, slow and sleepy, and the light came through her nightdress like sand through a sieve.

'Nothing's happening,' she said.

'Yes it is then,' I said. 'They're falling to bits.'

Dorothy scratched her dark head, yawning wide, and white feathers floated out of her hair.

'It's only the leaves droppin'. We're in autumn now. The leaves always drop in autumn.'

Autumn? In autumn. Was that where we were? Where the leaves always dropped and there was always this smell. I imagined it continuing, with no change, for ever, these wet flames of woods burning on and on like the bush of Moses, as natural a part of this new

13

found land as the eternal snows of the poles. Why had we come to such a place?

Marjorie, who had gone down to help with the breakfast, suddenly came tumbling back up the stairs.

'Doth,' she whispered; she seemed excited and frightened; 'Doth . . . 'e's turned up again. 'Elp on Loll with 'is clothes and come on down, quick.'

We went down and found him sitting by the fireside, smiling, wet and cold. I climbed up to the breakfast table and stared at him, the stranger. To me he did not so much appear to be a man as a conglomeration of woody things. His face was red and crinkled, brilliant like fungus. There were leaves in his mud-matted hair, and leaves and twigs on his crumbling clothes, and all over him. His boots were like the black pulp you find when you dig under a tree. Mother gave him porridge and bread, and he smiled palely at us all.

'It must have been cruel in the wood,' said our Mother.

'I've got some sacks, mam,' he said, spooning his porridge. 'They keep out the wet.'

They wouldn't; they'd suck it up like a wick and wrap him in it.

'You oughtn't to live like that,' said Mother. 'You ought to get back to your home.'

'No,' smiled the man. 'That wouldn't do. They'd jump on me before you could say knife.'

Mother shook her head sadly, and sighed, and gave him more porridge. We boys adored the look of the man; the girls, fastidious, were more uncertain of him. But he was no tramp or he wouldn't be in the kitchen. He had four bright medals in his pocket, which he would produce and polish and lay on the table like money. He spoke like nobody else we knew, in fact, we couldn't understand many of his words. But Mother seemed to understand him, and would ask him questions, and look at the photographs he carried in his shirt and sigh and shake her head. He talked something of battles and of flying in the air, and it was all wonderful to us.

He was no man from these parts. He had appeared on the doorstep one early morning, asking for a cup of tea. Our Mother had brought him in and given him a whole breakfast. There had been blood on his face and he had seemed very weak. Now he was in a kitchen with a woman and a lot of children, and his eyes shone brightly, and his whiskers smiled. He told us he was sleeping in the wood, which seemed to me a good idea. And he was a soldier, because Mother had said so.

I knew about war; all my uncles were in it; my ears from birth had been full of the talk of it. Sometimes I used to climb into the basket chair by the fire and close my eyes and see brown men moving over a field in battle. I was three, but I saw them grope and die and felt myself older than they.

This man did not look like a soldier. He was not brassoed, leather-belted and wax-whiskered like my uncles. He had a beard and his khaki was torn. But the girls insisted he was a soldier, and said it in whispers, like a secret. And when he came down to our house for breakfast, and sat hunched by the fire, steaming with damp and coated with leaves and dirt, I thought of him sleeping up there in the wood. I imagined him sleeping, then having a go at the battle, then coming down to us for a cup of tea. He was the war, and the war was up there; I wanted to ask, 'How's the war in that wood?'

But he never told us. He sat drinking his tea, gulping and gasping, the fire drawing the damp out of his clothes as if ghosts were rising from him. When he caught our eyes he smiled from his beard. And when brother Jack shot at him with a spoon, saying, 'I'm a sodger,' he replied softly, 'Aye, and you'd make a better

16

one than me, son, any day.'

When he said that, I wondered what had happened to the war. Was he in those rags because he was such a bad soldier? Had he lost the war in the wood?

When he didn't come any more, I knew he had. The girls said some policemen had taken him away in a cart. And Mother sighed and was sad over the poor man.

★   ★   ★

In weather that was new to me, and cold, and loud with bullying winds, my Mother disappeared to visit my father. This was a long way off, out of sight, and I don't remember her going. But suddenly there were only the girls in the house, tumbling about with brooms and dishcloths, arguing, quarrelling and putting us to bed at random. House and food had a new smell, and meals appeared like dismal conjuring tricks, cold, raw, or black with too much fire. Marjorie was breathless and everywhere; she was fourteen, with all the family in her care. My socks slipped down, and stayed down. I went unwashed for long periods of time. Black leaves swept into the house and piled up in the corners; it rained, and the floors sweated, and

17

washing filled all the lines in the kitchen and dripped sadly on one and all.

But we ate; and the girls moved about in a giggling flurry, exhausted at their losing game. As the days went by, such a tide of muddles mounted in the house that I didn't know which room was which. I lived free, grubbing outside in the mud till I was black as a badger. And my nose ran free, as unchecked as my feet. I sailed my boots down the drain, I cut up sheets for puttees and marched like a soldier through the swamps of leaves. Sensing my chance, I wandered far, eating all manner of raw objects, coloured berries, twigs and grubs, sick every day, but with a sickness of which I was proud.

All this time the sisters went through the house, darting upstairs and down, beset on all sides by the rain coming in, boys growing filthier, sheets scorching, saucepans burning and kettles boiling over. The doll's-house became a mad house, and the girls frail birds flying in a wind of chaos. Doth giggled helplessly, Phyl wept among the vegetables, and Marjorie would say, when the day was over, 'I'd lie down and die, if there was a place to lie down in.'

I was not at all surprised when I heard of the end of the world. Everything pointed to it.

The sky was low and whirling with black clouds; the wood roared night and day, stirring great seas of sound. One night we sat round the kitchen table, cracking walnuts with the best brass candlestick, when Marjorie came in from the town. She was shining with rain and loaded with bread and buns. She was also very white.

'The war's over,' she said. 'It's ended.'

'Never,' said Dorothy.

'They told me at the Stores,' said Marjorie. 'And they were giving away prunes.' She gave us a bagful, and we ate them raw.

The girls got tea and talked about it. And I was sure it was the end of the world. All my life was the war, and the war was the world. Now the war was over. So the end of the world was come. It made no other sense to me.

'Let's go out and see what's happening,' said Doth.

'You know we can't leave the kids,' Marge said.

So we went too. It was dark, and the gleaming roofs of the village echoed with the buzz of singing. We went hand in hand through the rain, up the bank and down the street. A bonfire crackled in one of the gardens, and a woman jumped up and down in the light of it, red as a devil, a jug in her hand, uttering cries

19

that were not singing. All down the other gardens there were other bonfires too. And a man came up and kissed the girls and hopped in the road and twisted on one toe. Then he fell down in the mud and lay there, working his legs like a frog and croaking a loud song.

I wanted to stop. I had never seen a man like this, in such a wild good humour. But we hurried on. We got to the pub and stared through the windows. The bar seemed on fire with its many lamps. Rose-coloured men, through the rain-wet windows, seemed to bulge and break into flame. They breathed out smoke, drank fire from golden jars, and I heard their great din with awe. Now anything might happen. And it did. A man rose up and crushed a glass like a nut between his hands, then held them out laughing for all to see his wounds. But the blood was lost in the general light of blood. Two other men came waltzing out of the door, locked in each other's arms. Fighting and cursing, they fell over the wall and rolled down the bank in the dark.

There was a screaming woman we could not see. 'Jimmy! Jimmy' she wailed. 'Oh, Jimmy! Thee s'll kill 'im! I'll fetch the vicar, I will! Oh, Jimmy!'

'Just 'ark at 'em,' said Dorothy, shocked and delighted.

'The kids ought to be in bed,' said Marjorie.

'Stop a minute longer. Only a minute. It wouldn't do no 'arm.'

Then the schoolhouse chimney caught on fire. A fountain of sparks shot high into the night, writhing and sweeping on the wind, falling and dancing along the road. The chimney hissed like a firework, great rockets of flame came gushing forth, emptying the tiny house, so that I expected to see chairs and tables, knives and forks, radiant and burning, follow. The moss-tiles smouldered with sulphurous soot, yellow jets of smoke belched from cracks in the chimney. We stood in the rain and watched it entranced, as if the sight had been saved for this day. As if the house had been saved, together with the year's bad litter, to be sent up in flames and rejoicing.

How everyone bellowed and scuffled and sang, drunk with their beer and the sight of the fire. But what would happen now that the war was over? What would happen to my uncles who lived in it?—those huge remote men who appeared suddenly at our house, reeking of leather and horses. What would happen to our father, who was khakied like every other man, yet special, not like other men? His picture hung over the piano, trim,

21

haughty, with a badged cap and a spiked moustache. I confused him with the Kaiser. Would he die now the war was over?

As we gazed at the flaming schoolhouse chimney, and smelt the burning throughout the valley, I knew something momentous was occurring. At any moment I looked for a spectacular end to my already long life. Oh, the end of the war and the world! There was rain in my shoes, and Mother had disappeared. I never expected to see another day.

FIRST NAMES

PEACE was here; but I could tell no difference. Our Mother returned from far away with excited tales of its madness, of how strangers had stopped and kissed each other in the streets and climbed statues shouting its name. But what was peace anyway? Food tasted the same, pump water was as cold, the house neither fell nor grew larger. Winter came in with a dark, hungry sadness, and the village filled up with unknown men who stood around in their braces and khaki pants, smoking short pipes, scratching their arms, and gazing in silence at the gardens.

I could not believe in this peace at all. It brought no angels or explanations; it had not altered the nature of my days and nights, nor gilded the mud in the yard. So I soon forgot it and went back to my burrowing among the mysteries of indoors and out. The garden still offered its corners of weed, blackened cabbages, its stones and flower-stalks. And the house its areas of hot and cold, dark holes and talking boards, its districts of terror and blessed sanctuary; together with an infinite range of objects and ornaments that folded, fastened, creaked and sighed, opened and shut, tinkled and sang, pinched, scratched, cut, burned, spun, toppled or fell to pieces. There was also a pepper-smelling cupboard, a ringing cellar and a humming piano, dry bunches of spiders, colliding brothers, and the eternal comfort of the women.

I was still young enough then to be sleeping with my Mother, which to me seemed life's whole purpose. We slept together in the first-floor bedroom on a flock-filled mattress in a bed of brass rods and curtains. Alone, at that time, of all the family, I was her chosen dream companion, chosen from all for her extra love; my right, so it seemed to me.

So in the ample night and the thickness of her hair I consumed my fattened sleep, drowsed and nuzzling to her warmth of flesh, blessed by her bed and safety. From the width of the house and the separation of the day, we two then lay joined alone. That darkness to me was like the fruit of sloes, heavy and ripe to the touch. It was a darkness of bliss and simple langour, when all edges seemed round-ed, apt and fitting; and the presence for whom one had moaned and hungered was found not to have fled after all.

My Mother, freed from her noisy day, would sleep like a happy child, humped in her

24

nightdress, breathing innocently, and making soft drinking sounds in the pillow. In her flights of dream she held me close, like a parachute to her back; or rolled and enclosed me with her great tired body so that I was snug as a mouse in a hayrick.

They were deep and jealous, those wordless nights, as we curled and muttered together, like a secret I held through the waking day which set me above all others. It was for me alone that the night came down, for me the prince of her darkness, when only I would know the huge helplessness of her sleep, her dead face and her blind bare arms. At dawn, when she rose and stumbled back to the kitchen, even then I was not wholly deserted, but rolled into the valley her sleep had left, lay deep in its smell of lavender, deep on my face to sleep again in the nest she had made my own.

The sharing of her bed at that three-year-old time I expected to last for ever. I had never known, or could not recall, any night spent away from her. But I was growing fast; I was no longer the baby; brother Tony lay in wait in his cot. When I heard the first whispers of moving me to the boys' room, I simply couldn't believe it. Surely my Mother would never agree? How could she face night without me?

My sisters began by soothing and flattering; they said, 'You're a grown big man.' 'You'll be sleeping with Harold and Jack,' they said. 'Now what d'you think of that?' What was I supposed to think?—to me it seemed outrageous. I affected a brainstorm and won a few extra nights, my last nights in that downy bed. Then the girls changed their tune: 'It'll only be for a bit. You can come back to Mum later on.' I didn't quite believe them, but Mother was silent, so I gave up the struggle and went.

I was never recalled to my Mother's bed again. It was my first betrayal, my first dose of aging hardness, my first lesson in the gentle, merciless rejection of women. Nothing more was said, and I accepted it. I grew a little tougher, a little colder, and turned my attention more towards the outside world, which by now was emerging visibly through the mist. . . .

★   ★   ★

The yard and the village manifested themselves at first through magic and fear. Projections of their spirits and of my hallucinations sketched in the first blanks with demons. The

26

thumping of heart-beats which I heard in my head was no longer the unique ticking of a private clock but the marching of monsters coming in from outside. They were creatures of the 'world' and they were coming for me, advancing up the valley with their heads stuck in bread-baskets, grunting to the thump of my blood. I suppose they were a result of early headaches, but I spent anxious days awaiting them. Indefatigable marchers though they were, they never got nearer than the edge of the village.

This was a daylight uneasiness which I shared with no one; but night, of course, held various others about which I was far more complaining—dying candles, doors closed on darkness, faces seen upside down, night holes in the ground where imagination seethed and sent one shrieking one's chattering head off. There were the Old Men too, who lived in the walls, in floors and down the lavatory; who watched and judged us and were pitilessly spiteful, and were obviously gods gone mouldy. These Old Men never failed to control us boys, and our sisters conjured them shamelessly, and indeed in a house where no father ruled they were the perfect surrogates.

But there was one real old pagan of flesh and blood who ruled us all for a while. His

27

visits to the village were rare yet deliberate; and when he appeared it was something both sovereign and evil that walked among us, though it was the women who were most clearly affected.

The first time I actually saw him myself had a salt-taste I still remember. It was a frost-bright, moon-cold night of winter, and we were sitting in the kitchen as usual. The fire boiled softly, the candles quivered, the girls were drowsily gossiping. I had fallen half-asleep across the table, when Marjorie suddenly said, 'Ssssh! . . .'

She had heard something of course, somebody was always hearing something, so I woke up and listened vaguely. The others were in attitudes of painful attention; they would listen at the drop of a feather. I heard nothing at first. An owl cried in the yew trees and was answered from another wood. Then Dorothy said 'Hark!' and Mother said 'Hush!' and the alarm had us all in its grip.

Like a stagless herd of hinds and young our heads all went up together. We heard it then, faraway down the lane, still faint and un-mistakable—the drag of metal on frost ground and an intermittent rattle of chains.

The girls exchanged looks of awful know-ledge, their bright eyes large with doom. 'It's

28

him!' they whispered in shaky voices. 'He's broke out again! It's him!'

It was him all right. Mother bolted the door and blew out the lamps and candles. Then we huddled together in the fire-flushed darkness to await his ominous coming.

The drag of the chains grew louder and nearer, rattling along the night, sliding towards us up the distant lane to his remorseless, moonlit tread. The girls squirmed in their chairs and began giggling horribly; they appeared to have gone off their heads.

'Hush,' warned our Mother. 'Keep quiet. Don't move. . . .' Her face was screwed in alarm.

The girls hung their heads and waited, shivering. The chains rattled nearer and nearer. Up the lane, round the corner, along the top of the bank—then with a drumming of feet, he was here. . . . Frantic, the girls could hold out no longer, they leapt up with curious cries, stumbled their way across the firelit kitchen and clawed the dark curtains back. . . .

Proud in the night the beast passed by, head crowned by royal horns, his milky eyes split by strokes of moonlight, his great frame shaggy with hair. He moved with stiff and stilted strides, swinging his silvered beard, and from the tangled strength of his thighs

29

and shoulders trailed the heavy chains he'd broken.

'Jones's goat!—' our Dorothy whispered; two words that were almost worship. For this was not just a straying animal but a beast of ancient dream, the moonlight-walker of the village roads, half captive, half rutting king. He was huge and hairy as a Shetland horse and all men were afraid of him; Squire Jones in fact kept him chained to a spike driven five feet into the ground. Yet when nights were bright with moon or summer neither spike nor chains could hold him. Then he snorted and reared, tore his chains from the ground, and came trailing his lust through the village.

I had heard of him often; now I saw him at last, striding jerkily down the street. Old as a god, wearing his chains like a robe, he exuded a sharp whiff of salt, and every few steps he sniffed at the air as though seeking some friend or victim. But he walked alone; he encountered no one, he passed through an empty village. Daughters and wives peeped from darkened bedrooms, men waited in the shadows with axes. Meanwhile, reeking with power and white in the moon, he went his awesome way. . . .

'Did you ever see a goat so big?' asked Dorothy with a sigh.

'They knocks you down and tramples you. I heard he knocked down Miss Cohen.'

'Just think of meeting him coming home alone. . . .'

'Whatever would you do?'

'I'd have a fit. What would you do Phyl?'

Phyl didn't answer: she had run away, and was having hysterics in the pantry.

★   ★   ★

Jones's terrorist goat seemed to me a natural phenomenon of that time, part of a village which cast up beasts and spirits as casually as human beings. All seemed part of the same community, though their properties varied widely—some were benevolent, some strictly to be avoided; there were those that appeared at different shapes of the moon, or at daylight or midnight hours, that could warn or bless or drive one mad according to their different natures. There was the Death Bird, the Coach, Miss Barraclough's Goose, Hangman's House, and the Two-Headed Sheep.

There is little remarkable about a two-headed sheep, except that this one was old and talked English. It lived alone among the Catswood Larches, and was only visible during flashes of lightning. It could sing harmoniously in a double voice and cross-question itself for hours; many travellers had heard it when passing that wood, but few, naturally enough, had seen it. Should a thunderstorm ever have confronted you with it, and had you had the presence of mind to enquire, it would have told you the date and nature of your death—at least so people said. But no one quite relished the powers of this beast. And when the sheep-lightning flickered over the Catswood trees it was thought best to keep away from the place.

The Bulls Cross Coach was another ill omen, and a regular midnight visitor. Bulls Cross was a saddle of heathland set high at the end of the valley, once a crossing of stage-roads and cattle-tracks which joined Berkeley to Birdlip, and Bisley to Gloucester-Market. Relics of the old stage-roads still imprinted the grass as well as the memories of the older villagers. And up here, any midnight, but particularly New Year's Eve, one could see a silver-grey coach drawn by flaring horses thundering out of control, could hear the pistol crack of snapping harness, the screams of the passengers, the splintering of wood and the coachman's desperate cries. The vision recalled some ancient disaster, and was

32

rehearsed every night, at midnight.

Those who hadn't seen it boasted they had, but those who had seen it, never. For the sight laid a curse upon talkative witnesses, a curse we all believed in—you went white in the night, and your teeth fell out, and later you died by trampling. So news of the phantom usually came second-hand. 'They sin that coach agen last night. 'Arry Lazbury sin it, they says. He was comin' from Painsick a-pushin' 'is bike. 'E dropped it, an' run 'ome crazy.' We committed poor Harry to his horrible end, while the Coach ran again through our minds, gliding white on its rocking wheels, as regular as the Post.

As for the tiny tragedy behind the phantom, it had been jealously remembered to haunt us. The tilted coach, the splintered shafts, the wheels crooked against the moon, the sobbing horses kicking out each other's brains, the passengers dying on the moor—the image of that small but local disaster still possessed qualities to appal which the more grandiose carnage of recent times has never quite overshadowed.

As for Bulls Cross—that ragged wildness of wind-bent turves—I still wouldn't walk there at midnight. It was a curious tundra, a sort of island of nothing set high above the

33

crowded valleys. Yet its hollows and silences, bare of all habitations, seemed stained by the encounters of strangers. At this no-man's-crossing, in the days of footpads and horses, travellers would meet in suspicion, or lie in wait to do violence on each other, to rob or rape or murder. To the villages around, it was a patch of bare skyline, a baldness among the woods, a wind-scarred platform which caught everybody's eye, and was therefore just the place for a gibbet. A gibbet, consequently, had stood there for years, which the old folk could still remember.

Below Bulls Cross stood a dank yellow wood which we knew as Deadcombe Bottom. My brothers and I discovered a cottage down there, roof-fallen, in a garden run wild. We played there often among its rotting rooms, running up the littered stairs, picking and gorging on the small sharp apples which hung round the shattered windows. It was a damp dark ruin in the damp depth of the wood; its rooms reeked of old beds and fungus. And behind the door, blood-red with rust, hung a naked iron hook.

To this silent, birdless, sunless shambles we returned again and again. We could do what we liked here, wreak what damage we wished, and strangely enough no one disturbed us.

Only later did we learn the history of the place: that it had been the home of the Bulls Cross hangman, that he had lived here with his son, and worked at his trade, and had later killed himself here.

The cottage in the wood had been specially chosen, close to his work, yet hidden. The times were hungry, his days were busy; he was a discreet and skilful man. Night after night he strolled up the hill to load the gallows with local felons. After a routine summons one storm-black evening, he was handed a shivering boy. Used to working in darkness, he dispatched the lad quickly, then paused to light up his pipe. He was turning to go when a cloud moved from the moon and lit up the gallows clearly, and in the rain-washed face that stared crookedly down at him the hangman saw his son. To the men who stood by he said nothing at all. He just walked back to his cottage, drove a hook into the wall, fixed up a noose and hanged himself.

Since when no one had lived in Hangman's House, which crumbled in Deadcombe Bottom, where we played, and chewed apples, and swung from that hook, and kicked the damp walls to pieces. . . .

★   ★   ★

35

From the age of five or so I began to grow acquainted with several neighbours —outlaws most of them in dress and behaviour —whom I remember both by name and deed. There was Cabbage-Stump Charlie, Albert the Devil, and Percy-from-Painswick, to begin with.

Cabbage-Stump Charlie was our local bruiser—a violent, gaitered, gaunt-faced pigman, who lived only for his sows and for fighting. He was a nourisher of quarrels, as some men are of plants, growing them from nothing by the heat of belligerence and watering them daily with blood. He would set out each evening, armed with his cabbage-stalk, ready to strike down the first man he saw. 'What's up then, Charlie? Got no quarrel with thee.' 'Wham!' said Charlie, and hit him. Men fell from their bicycles or back-pedalled violently when they saw old Charlie coming. With his hawk-brown nose and whiskered arms he looked like a land-locked Viking; and he would take up his stand outside the pub, swing his great stump round his head, and say 'Wham! Bash!' like a boy in a comic, and challenge all comers to battle. Often bloodied himself, he left many a man bleeding before crawling back home to his

36

pigs. Cabbage-Stump Charlie, like Jones's Goat, set the village to bolting its doors.

Albert the Devil was another alarmer—a deaf-mute beggar with a black beetle's body, short legs, and a mouth like a puppet's. He had soft-boiled eyes of unusual power which filled every soul with disquiet. It was said he could ruin a girl with a glance and take the manhood away from a man, or scramble your brains, turn bacon green and effect other domestic disorders. So when he came to the village on a begging trip, and we heard his musical gurgle approaching, money and food was put on the tops of the walls and then people shut themselves up in their privies.

Percy-from-Painswick, on the other hand, was a clown and a ragged dandy, who used to come over the hill, dressed in frock-coat and leggings, looking for local girls. Harmless, half-witted, he wooed only with his tongue; but his words were sufficient to befuddle the girls and set them shrieking with pleasure and shock. He had a sharp pink face and a dancer's light body and the girls used to follow him everywhere, teasing him on into cheekier fancies and pinning ribbons to his swallow-tail coat. Then he'd spin on his toes, and say something quick and elaborate, uttered smoothly from smiling teeth—and the girls would run screaming down over the bank, red-faced, excited, incredulous, hiding in bushes to exclaim to each other was it possible what Percy just said? He was a gentle, sharp, sweet-moving man, but he died of his brain soon after.

Then there was Willy the Fish, who came round on Fridays, mongering from door to door, with baskets of mackerel of such antiquity that not even my family could eat them. Willy was a loose-lipped, sad-eyed man who had lost his girl to his trade. He would lean by our door, and blow and scratch, and lament how it was he'd lost her. But transport was bad, and the sea far away; and the truth was poor Willy stank.

Among others I remember was Tusker Tom, who sold sacks of tree-roots for burning. And Harelip Harry, Davis the Drag, Fisty Fill, and the Prospect Smiler. The first-named three were orbiting tramps, but the last was a manic farmer. Few men I think can have been as unfortunate as he; for on the one hand he was a melancholic with a loathing for mankind, on the other, some paralysis had twisted his mouth into a permanent and radiant smile. So everyone he met, being warmed by this smile, would shout him a happy greeting. And beaming upon them with his sunny face

38

he would curse them all to hell.

Bulls Cross itself had two daylight familiars: John-Jack and Emmanuel Twinning. John-Jack spent his time by the Bulls Cross signpost staring gloomily into Wales. Silent, savage, with a Russian look, he lived with his sister Nancy, who had borne him over the course of years five children of remarkable beauty. Emmanuel Twinning on the other hand, was gentle and very old, and made his own suits out of hospital blankets, and lived nearby with a horse.

Emmanuel and the skewbald had much in common, including the use of the kitchen, and one saw their grey heads, almost any evening, poking together out of the window. The old man himself, when seen alone, seemed to inhabit unearthly regions, so blue and remote that the girls used to sing:

O come, O come, E-mah-ah-ah-new-el!
An' ransom captive Is-rah-ah-ah-el! . . .

At this he would nod and smile gently upon us, moving his lips to the hymn. He was so very old, so far and strange, I never doubted that the hymn was his. He wore sky-blue blankets, and his name was Emmanuel; it was easy to think he was God.

39

*   *   *

In the long hot summer of 1921 a serious
drought hit the country. Springs dried up, the
wells filled with frogs, and the usually sweet
water from our scullery pump turned brown
and tasted of nails. Although this drought was
a relief to my family, it was a scourge to the
rest of the village. For weeks the sky hung hot
and blue, trees shrivelled, crops burned in the
fields, and the old folk said the sun had
slipped in its course and that we should all of
us very soon die. There were prayers for rain;
but my family didn't go, because it was rain
we feared most of all.

As the drought continued, prayer was
abandoned and more devilish steps adopted.
Finally soldiers with rifles marched to the
tops of the hills and began shooting at passing
clouds. When I heard their dry volleys, break-
ing like sticks in the stillness, I knew our long
armistice was over. And sure enough—
whether from prayers or the shooting, or by a
simple return of nature—the drought broke
soon after and it began to rain as it had never
rained before.

I remember waking in the night to the
screams of our Mother, and to rousing alarms

40

of a howling darkness and the storm-battered trees outside. Terror, the old terror, had come again, and as always in the middle of the night.

'Get up!' cried Mother. 'It's coming in! Get up or we'll all be drowned!'

I heard her banging about and beating the walls in accents of final doom. When Mother gave her alarms one didn't lie back and think, one didn't use reason at all; one just erected one's hair and leapt out of bed and scrambled downstairs with the others.

Our predicament was such that we lived at nature's mercy; for the cottage, stuck on its steep bank, stood directly in the path of the floods. All the spouts of the heavens seemed to lead to our door, and there was only one small drain to swallow them. When this drain blocked up, as it did in an instant, the floods poured into our kitchen—and as there was no back door to let them out again I felt it natural at the time we should drown.

'Hell in Heaven!' wailed Mother. 'Damn it and cuss! Jesus have mercy on us!'

We grizzled and darted about for brooms, then ran out to tackle the storm. We found the drain blocked already and the yard full of water. The noise of the rain drowned our cries and whimpers, and there was nothing to do

41

but sweep.

What panic those middle-night rousings were, those trumpet-calls murdering sleep; with darkness, whirlwind and invisible rain, trees roaring, clouds bursting, thunder crashing, lightning crackling, floods rising and our Mother demented. The girls in their night-dresses held spitting candles while we boys swept away at the drain. Hot rods of rain struck straight through our shirts; we shivered with panic and cold.

'More brooms!' shouted Mother, jumping up and down. 'Run, someone, in the name of goodness! Sweep harder, boys! Sweet saints above, it's up to the doorstep already!'

The flood-water gurgled and moved thickly around us, breeding fat yellow bubbles like scum, skipping and frothing where the bullet rain hit it and inching slowly towards the door. The drain was now hidden beneath the water and we swept at it for our lives, the wet candles hissed and went out one by one, Mother lit torches of newspapers, while we fought knee-deep in cries and thunder, splashing about, wet-through, half-weeping, overwhelmed by gigantic fears.

Sometimes, in fact, the water did get in; two or three inches of it. It slid down the steps like a thick cream custard and spread all over the floor. When that happened, Mother's lamentations reached elegiac proportions, and all the world was subpœnaed to witness. Dramatic apostrophes rang through the night; the Gods were arraigned, the Saints called to order, and the Fates severely ticked off.

There would be a horrible mess in the kitchen next morning, mud and slime all over the matting, followed by the long depressed drudgery of scraping it up and carrying it away in buckets. Mother, on her knees, would ring her hands and roll her eyes about.

'I can't *think* what I've done to be so troubled and tried. And just when I got the house straight. Neither saints nor angels would keep their patience if they had such things to put up with. . . . My poor, poor children, my precious darlings—you could die in this filthy hole. No one would care—not a bell-essed soul. Look out with that damn-and-cuss bucket!' . . .

Apart from the noise and the tears and the dirt, these inundations were really not much. But I can't pretend they didn't scare me stiff. The thought that the flood-waters should actually break into our house seemed to me something worse than a fire. At the mid-hour of night, when the storms really blew, I used

43

to lie aghast in my bed, hearing the rain claw the window and the wind slap the walls, and imagining the family, the house, and all the furniture, being sucked down the eternal drain.

It was not till much later that I reasoned things out: that our position on the hillside made it unlikely we should drown, that Mother's frenzies and scares belonged to something else altogether, and that it was possible after all to sleep through rain in peace. Even so, to this day, when the skies suddenly darken, and a storm builds up in the west, and I smell rain on the wind and hear the first growl of thunder, I grow uneasy, and start looking for brooms.

VILLAGE SCHOOL

THE village to which our family had come was a scattering of some twenty to thirty houses down the south-east slope of a valley. The valley was narrow, steep and almost entirely cut off; it was also a funnel for winds, a channel for the floods, and a jungley, bird-crammed, insect-hopping sun-trap whenever there happened to be any sun. It was not high and open like the Windrush country, but had secret origins, having been gouged from the Escarpment by the melting ice-caps some time before we got there. The old flood-terraces still showed on the slopes, along which the cows walked sideways. Like an island, it was possessed of curious survivals—rare orchids and Roman snails; and there were chemical qualities in the limestone-springs which gave the women pre-Raphaelite goitres. The sides of the valley were rich in pasture and the crests heavily covered in beechwoods.

Living down there was like living in a beanpod; one could see nothing but the bed one lay in. Our horizon of woods was the limit of our world. For weeks on end the trees moved in the wind with a dry roaring that seemed a natural utterance of the landscape. In winter they ringed us with frozen spikes, and in summer they oozed over the lips of the hills like layers of thick green lava. Mornings, they steamed with mist or sunshine, and almost every evening threw streamers above us, reflecting sunsets we were too hidden to see.

Water was the most active thing in the valley, arriving in the long rains from Wales. It would drip all day from clouds and trees, from roofs and eaves and noses. It broke open roads, carved its way through gardens, and filled the ditches with sucking noises. Men and horses walked about in wet sacking, birds shook rainbows from sodden branches, and streams ran from holes, and back into holes, like noisy underground trains.

I remember, too, the light on the slopes, long shadows in tufts and hollows, with cattle, brilliant as painted china, treading their echoing shapes. Bees blew like cake-crumbs through the golden air, white butterflies like sugared wafers, and when it wasn't raining a diamond dust took over which veiled and yet magnified all things.

Most of the cottages were built of Cotswold stone and were roofed by split-stone tiles. The tiles grew a kind of golden moss

46

which sparkled like crystallized honey. Behind the cottages were long steep gardens full of cabbages, fruit-bushes, roses, rabbit-hutches, earth-closets, bicycles and pigeon-lofts. In the very sump of the valley wallowed the Squire's Big House—once a fine, though modest sixteenth-century manor, to which a Georgian façade had been added.

The villagers themselves had three ways of living: working for the Squire, or on the farms, or down in the cloth-mills at Stroud. Apart from the Manor, and the ample cottage gardens—which were an insurance against hard times—all other needs were supplied by a church, a chapel, a vicarage, a manse, a wooden hut, a pub—and the village school.

*   *   *

The village school at that time provided all the instruction we were likely to ask for. It was a small stone barn divided by a wooden partition into two rooms—The Infants and The Big Ones. There was one dame teacher, and perhaps a young girl assistant. Every child in the valley came crowding there, remained till he was fourteen years old, then was presented to the working field or factory with nothing in his head more burdensome than a few mnemonics, a jumbled list of wars and a dreamy image of the world's geography. It seemed enough to get by with, in any case; and was one up on our poor old grandparents.

This school, when I came to it, was at its peak. Universal education and unusual fertility had packed it to the walls with pupils. Wild boys and girls from miles around—from the outlying farms and half-hidden hovels way up at the ends of the valley—swept down each day to add to our numbers, bringing with them strange oaths and odours, quaint garments and curious pies. They were my first amazed vision of any world outside the womanly warmth of my family; I didn't expect to survive it for long, and I was confronted with it at the age of four.

The morning came, without any warning, when my sisters surrounded me, wrapped me in scarves, tied up my boot-laces, thrust a cap on my head, and stuffed a baked potato in my pocket.

'What's this?' I said.

'You're starting school today.'

'I ain't. I'm stopping 'ome.'

'Now, come on, Loll. You're a big boy now.'

'I ain't.'

'You are.'

'Boo-hoo.'

They picked me up bodily, kicking and bawling, and carried me up to the road.

'Boys who don't go to school get put into boxes, and turn into rabbits, and get chopped up Sundays.'

I felt this was overdoing it rather, but I said no more after that. I arrived at the school just three feet tall and fatly wrapped in my scarves. The playground roared like a rodeo, and the potato burned through my thigh. Old boots, ragged stockings, torn trousers and skirts, went skating and skidding around me. The rabble closed in; I was encircled; grit flew in my face like shrapnel. Tall girls with frizzled hair, and huge boys with sharp elbows, began to prod me with hideous interest. They plucked at my scarves, spun me round like a top, screwed my nose and stole my potato.

I was rescued at last by a gracious lady— the sixteen-year-old junior-teacher—who boxed a few ears and dried my face and led me off to The Infants. I spent that first day picking holes in paper, then went home in a smouldering temper.

'What's the matter, Loll? Didn't he like it at school, then?'

'They never gave me the present!'

'Present? What present?'

'They said they'd give me a present.'

'Well, now, I'm sure they didn't.'

'They did! They said: "You're Laurie Lee, ain't you? Well, just you sit there for the present." I sat there all day but I never got it. I ain't going back there again!'

But after a week I felt like a veteran and grew as ruthless as anyone else. Somebody had stolen my baked potato, so I swiped somebody else's apple. The Infant Room was packed with toys such as I'd never seen before—coloured shapes and rolls of clay, stuffed birds and men to paint. Also a frame of counting beads which our young teacher played like a harp, leaning her bosom against our faces and guiding our wandering fingers. . . .

*   *   *

The beautiful assistant left us at last, and was replaced by an opulent widow. She was tall, and smelt like a cartload of lavender; and wore a hair net, which I thought was a wig. I remember going close up and having a good look—it was clearly too square to be hair.

'What are you staring at?' the widow enquired.

I was much too soft-hearted to answer.

'Go on. Do tell. You needn't be shy.'

'You're wearing a wig,' I said.

'I can assure you I'm not!' She went very red.

'You are. I seen it.' I said.

The new teacher grew flustered and curiously cross. She took me upon her knee.

'Now look very close. Is that really a wig?'

I looked hard, saw the net, and said, 'Yes.'

'Well, really!' she said, while the Infants gaped. 'I can assure you it's *not* a wig! And if you only could watch me getting dressed in the morning you'd know it wasn't one either.'

She shook me from her knee like a sodden cat, but she'd stirred my imagination. To suggest I might watch her getting dressed in the morning seemed to me both outrageous and wonderful.

★   ★   ★

This tiny, white-washed Infants' room was a brief but cosy anarchy. In that short time allowed us we played and wept, broke things, fell asleep, cheeked the teacher, discovered the things we could do to each other, and exhaled our last guiltless days.

My desk companions were those two blonde girls, already puppyishly pretty, whose names and bodies were to distract and haunt me for the next fifteen years of my life. Poppy and Jo were limpet chums; they sat holding hands all day; and there was a female self-possession about their pink sticky faces that made me shout angrily at them.

Vera was another I studied and liked; she was lonely, fuzzy and short. I felt a curious compassion for stumpy Vera; and it was through her, and no beauty, that I got into trouble and received the first public shock of my life. How it happened was simple, and I was innocent, so it seemed. She came up to me in the playground one morning and held her face close to mine. I had a stick in my hand, so I hit her on the head with it. Her hair was springy, so I hit her again and watched her mouth open up with a yell.

To my surprise a commotion broke out around me, cries of scandal from the older girls, exclamations of horror and heavy censure mixed with Vera's sobbing wails. I was intrigued, not alarmed, that by wielding a beech stick I was able to cause such a stir. So I hit her again, without spite or passion, then walked off to try something else.

The experiment might have ended there, and having ended would have been forgotten. But no; angry faces surrounded me, very red, all spitting and scolding.

'Horrid boy! Poor Vera! Little monster! Urgh! We're going to tell teacher about you!'

Something was wrong, the world seemed upset, I began to feel vaguely uneasy. I had only hit Vera on her wiry black hair, and now everybody was shouting at me. I ran and hid, feeling sure it would pass, but they hunted me down in the end. Two big righteous girls hauled me out by the ears.

'You're wanted in the Big Room, for 'itting Vera. You're 'alf going to cop it!' they said.

So I was dragged to that Room, where I'd never been before, and under the savage eyes of the elder children teacher gave me a scalding lecture. I was confused by now and shaking with guilt. At last I smirked and ran out of the room. I had learnt my first lesson, that I could not hit Vera, no matter how fuzzy her hair. And something else too; that the summons to the Big Room, the policeman's hand on the shoulder, comes almost always as a complete surprise, and for the crime that one has forgotten.

⋆   ⋆   ⋆

My brother Jack, who was with me in the Infants, was too clever to stay there long.

53

Indeed, he was so bright he made us uncomfortable, and we were all of us glad to get rid of him. Sitting pale in his pinafore, gravely studying, commanding the teacher to bring him fresh books, or to sharpen his pencils, or to make less noise, he was an Infant Freak from the start. So he was promoted to the Big Room with unprecedented promptness, given a desk and a dozen atlases to sit on, from which he continued to bully the teachers in that cold clear voice of his.

But I, myself, was a natural Infant, content to serve out my time, to slop around and whine and idle; and no one suggested I shouldn't. So I remained long after bright Jack had moved on, the fat lord of my nursery life, skilled at cutting out men from paper, chalking suns on the walls, making snakes from clay, idling voluptuously through the milky days with a new young teacher to feed on. But my time was slowly running out; my Big Room bumps were growing. Suddenly, almost to my dismay, I found that I could count up to a hundred, could write my name in both large and small letters, and subtract certain numbers from each other. I had even just succeeded in subtracting Poppy from Jo, when the call came down from on high. Infant no longer, I was being moved up—the Big

54

Room was ready for me.

I found there a world both adult and tough, with long desks and inkwells, strange maps on the walls, huge boys, heavy boots, scratching pens, groans of labour, and sharp and sudden persecutions. Gone for ever were the infant excuses, the sanctuary of lisping charms. Now I was alone and unprotected, faced by a struggle which required new techniques, where one made pacts and split them, made friends and betrayed them, and fought for one's place near the stove.

The stove was a symbol of caste among us, the tub of warmth to which we cleaved during the long seven months of winter. It was made of cast-iron and had a noisy mouth which rattled coke and breathed out fumes. It was decorated by a tortoise labelled 'Slow But Sure', and in winter it turned red hot. If you pressed a pencil against it, the wood burst into flames; and if you spat on the top, the spit hopped and gambolled like tiny ping-pong balls.

My first days in the Big Room were spent in regret for the young teacher I'd left in the Infants, for her braided breasts and unbuttoning hands and her voice of sleepy love. Quite clearly the Big Room boasted no such comforts; Miss B, the Head Teacher, to whom I was now delivered, being about as physically soothing as a rake.

She was a bunched and punitive little body and the school had christened her Crabby; she had a sour yellow look, lank hair coiled in earphones, and the skin and voice of a turkey. We were all afraid of the gobbling Miss B; she spied, she pried, she crouched, she crept, she pounced—she was a terror.

Each morning was war without declaration; no one knew who would catch it next. We stood to attention, half-crippled in our desks, till Miss B walked in, whacked the walls with a ruler, and fixed us with her squinting eye. 'Good a-morning, children!' 'Good morning, Teacher!' The greeting was like a rattling of swords. Then she would scowl at the floor and begin to growl 'Ar Farther . . .'; at which we said the Lord's Prayer, praised all good things, and thanked God for the health of our King. But scarcely had we bellowed the last Amen than Crabby coiled, uncoiled and sprang, and knocked some poor boy sideways.

One seldom knew why; one was always off guard, for the punishment preceded the charge. The charge, however, followed hard upon it, to a light shower of angry spitting.

'Shuffling your feet! Playing with the desk! A-smirking at that miserable Betty! I will not

56

have it. I'll not, I say. I repeat—I will not have it!'

Many a punch-drunk boy in a playground battle, outnumbered and beaten to his knees, would be heard to cry: 'I will not have it! I'll not, I say! I repeats I will not have it!' It was an appeal to the code of our common suffering, and called for immediate mercy.

So we did not much approve of Crabby—though she was responsible for our excellent reflexes. Apart from this, her teaching was not memorable. She appears in my recollection as merely a militant figure, a hunched-up little creature all spring-coils and slaps—not a monster by any means, but a natural manifestation of what we expected of school.

For school in my day, that day, Crabby's day, seemed to be designed simply to keep us out of the air and from following the normal pursuits of the fields. Crabby's science of dates and sums and writing seemed a typical invention of her own, a sour form of fiddling or prison-labour like picking oakum or sewing sacks.

So while the bright times passed, we sat locked in our stocks, our bent backs turned on the valley. The June air infected us with primitive hungers, grass-seed and thistle-down idled through the windows, we smelt the fields and were tormented by cuckoos, while every out-of-door sound that came drifting in was a sharp nudge in the solar plexus. The creaking of wagons going past the school, harness-jingle and the cries of the carters, the calling of cows from the 17-Acre, Fletcher's chattering mower, gunshots from the warrens—all tugged and pulled at our active wishes till we could have done Miss B a murder.

And indeed there came the inevitable day when rebellion raised its standard, when the tension was broken and a hero emerged whom we would willingly have named streets after. At least, from that day his name was honoured, though we gave him little support at the time. . . .

Spadge Hopkins it was, and I must say we were surprised. He was one of those heavy, full-grown boys, thick-legged, red-fisted, bursting with flesh, designed for the great out-doors. He was nearly fourteen by then, and physically out of scale—at least so far as our school was concerned. The sight of him squeezed into his tiny desk was worse than a bullock in ballet-shoes. He wasn't much of a scholar; he groaned as he worked, or hacked at his desk with a jack-knife. Miss B took her pleasure in goading him, in forcing him to read out loud; or asking him sudden unintelligible questions which made him flush and stumble.

The great day came; a day of shimmering summer, with the valley outside in a state of leafy levitation. Crabby B was at her sourest, and Spadge Hopkins had had enough. He began to writhe in his desk, and roll his eyes, and kick with his boots, and mutter; 'She'd better look out. 'Er, — Crabby B. She'd better, that's all. I can tell you. . . .'

We didn't quite know what the matter was, in spite of his meaning looks. Then he threw down his pen, said; 'Sod it all,' got up and walked to the door.

'And where are you going, young man, may I ask?' said Crabby with her awful leer.

Spadge paused and looked her straight in the eye.

'If it's any business of yourn.'

We shivered with pleasure at this defiance, Spadge leisurely made for the door.

'Sit down this instant!' Crabby suddenly screamed. 'I won't have it!'

'Ta-ta,' said Spadge.

Then Crabby sprang like a yellow cat, spitting and clawing with rage. She caught Spadge in the doorway and fell upon him. There was a shameful moment of heavy breathing and scuffling, while the teacher tore at his clothes. Spadge caught her hands in his great red fists and held her at arm's length, struggling.

'Come and help me, someone!' wailed Crabby, demented. But nobody moved; we just watched. We saw Spadge lift her up and place her on the top of the cupboard, then walk out of the door and away. There was a moment of silence, then we all laid down our pens and began to stamp on the floor in unison. Crabby stayed where she was, on top of the cupboard, drumming her heels and weeping.

*   *   *

We expected some terrible retribution to follow, but nothing happened at all. Not even the trouble-spark, Spadge, was called to account—he was simply left alone. From that day Crabby never spoke to him, or crossed his path, or denied him anything at all. He perched idly in his desk, his knees up to his chin, whistling in a world of his own. Sometimes Miss B would consider him narrowly and if he caught her glance he just winked. Otherwise he was free to come and go, and to take time off as he pleased.

But we never rebelled again; things

changed. Crabby B was replaced by a new Head Teacher—a certain Miss Wardley from Birmingham. This lady was something quite new in our lives. She wore sharp glass jewellery which winked as she walked, and she sounded her 'gees' like gongs. But she was fond of singing and she was fond of birds, and she encouraged us in the study of both. She was more sober than Crabby, her reins looser but stronger; and after the first hilarity of her arrival and strangeness, we accepted her proper authority.

Not that she approved very much of me. 'Fat-and-Lazy', was the name she called me. After my midday dinner of baked cabbage and bread I would often nod off in my desk. 'Wake up!' she would cry, cracking my head with a ruler, 'you and your little red eyes!' She also took exception to my steady sniff, which to me came as natural as breathing. 'Go out into the road and have a good blow, and don't come back in till you're clear.' But I wouldn't blow, not for anyone on earth, especially if ordered to do so: so I'd sit out on the wall, indignant and thunderous, and sniff away louder than ever. I wouldn't budge either, or come back, till a boy was sent to fetch me. Miss Wardley would greet me with freezing brightness. 'A little less beastly now? How

61

about bringing a hanky tomorrow? I'm sure we'd all be grateful.' I'd sit and scowl, then forget to scowl, and would soon be asleep again. . . .

My brothers, by this time, were all with me at school. Jack, already the accepted genius, was long past our scope or help. It was agreed that his brains were of such distinction that they absolved him from mortal contacts. So he was left in a corner where his flashes of brilliance kept him twinkling away like a pin-table. Young Tony came last, but he again was different, being impervious either to learning or authority, importing moreover a kind of outrageous cheekiness so inspired that it remained unanswerable. He would sit all day picking holes in blotting paper, his large eyes deep and knowing, his quick tongue scandalous, his wit defiant, his will set against all instruction. There was nothing anyone could do about him, except to yelp at the things he said.

I alone, the drowsy middleman of these two, found it hard to win Miss Wardley's approval. I achieved this in the end by writing long faked essays on the lives and habits of otters. I'd never seen an otter, or even gone to look for one, but the essays took her in. They were read out aloud, and even earned me medals, but that's nothing to boast about.

★   ★   ★

Our village school was poor and crowded, but in the end I relished it. It had a lively reek of steaming life: boys' boots, girls' hair, stoves and sweat, blue ink, white chalk and shavings. We learnt nothing abstract or tenuous there—just simple patterns of facts and letters, portable tricks of calculation, no more than was needed to measure a shed, write out a bill, read a swine-disease warning. Through the dead hours of the morning, through the long afternoons, we chanted away at our tables. Passers-by could hear our rising voices in our bottled-up room on the bank: 'Twelve-inches-one-foot.   Three-feet-make-a-yard. Fourteen-pounds-make-a-stone. Eight-stone-a-hundred-weight.' We absorbed these figures as primal truths declared by some ultimate power. Unhearing, unquestioning, we rocked to our chanting, hammering the gold nails home. 'Twice-two-are-four.   One-God-is-Love.   One-Lord-is-King.   One-King-is-George. One-George-is-Fifth. . . .' So it was always; had been, would be for ever; we asked no questions; we didn't hear what we said; yet neither did we ever forget it.

So do I now, through the reiterations of those days, recall that schoolroom which I scarcely noticed—Miss Wardley in glory on her high desk throne, her long throat tinkling with glass. The bubbling stove with its chink of red fire; the old world map as dark as tea; dead field-flowers in jars on the windowsills; the cupboard yawning with dog-eared books. Then the boys and the girls, the dwarfs and the cripples; the slow fat ones and the quick boney ones; giants and louts, angels and squinters—Walt Kerry, Bill Timbrell, Spadge Hopkins, Clergy Green, the Ballingers and Browns, Betty Gleed, Clarry Hogg, Sam and Sixpence, Poppy and Jo—we were ugly and beautiful, scrofulous, warted, ringwormed and scabbed at the knees; we were noisy, crude, intolerant, cruel, stupid and superstitious. But we moved together out of the clutch of the Fates, inhabitors of a world without doom; with a scratching, licking and chewing of pens, a whisper and passing of jokes, a titter of tickling, a grumble of labour, a vague stare at the wall in a dream. . . .

'Oh, miss, please miss, can I go round the back?'

An unwilling nod permits me. I stamp out noisily into a swoop of fresh air and a musical surge of birds. All around me now is the free green world, with Mrs Birt hanging out her washing. I take stock of myself for a moment, alone. I hear the schoolroom's beehive hum. Of course I don't really belong to that lot at all; I know I'm something special, a young king perhaps placed secretly here in order to mix with the commoners. There is clearly a mystery about my birth, I feel so unique and majestic. One day, I know, the secret will be told. A coach with footmen will appear suddenly at our cottage, and Mother (my mother?) will weep. The family will stand very solemn and respectful, and I shall drive off to take up my throne. I'll be generous, of course, not proud at all; for my brothers there shall be no dungeons. Rather will I feed them on cakes and jellies, and I'll provide all my sisters with princes. Sovereign mercy shall be their portion, little though they deserve it. . . .

I return to the schoolroom and Miss Wardley scowls (she shall curtsy when I am king). But all this is forgotten when Walt Kerry leans over and demands the results of my sums. 'Yes, Walt. Of course, Walt. Here, copy them out. They ain't hard—I done 'em all.' He takes them, the bully, as his tributary right, and I'm proud enough to give them. Then little Jim Fern, sitting beside me, looks up from his ruined pages. 'Ain't you a good scholar! You and your Jack. I wish I was a good scholar like thee.' He gives me a sad, adoring look, and I begin to feel much better.

Playtime comes and we charge outdoors, releasing our steamed-up cries. Somebody punches a head. Somebody bloodies their knees. Boys cluster together like bees. 'Let's go round the back then, shall us, eh?' To the dark narrow alley, rich with our mysteries, we make our clattering way. Over the wall is the girl's own place, quite close, and we shout them greetings.

'I 'eard you, Bill Timbrell! I 'eard what you said! You be careful, I'll tell our teacher!'

Flushed and refreshed, we stream back to our playground, whistling, indivisibly male.

'D'you 'ear what I said then? Did you then, eh? *I* told 'em! They 'alf didn't squeal!'

We all double up; we can't speak for laughing, we can't laugh without hitting each other.

★   ★   ★

Miss Wardley was patient, but we weren't very bright. Our books showed a squalor of blots and scratches as though monkeys were being taught to write. We sang in sweet

66

choirs, and drew like cavemen, but most other faculties escaped us. Apart from poetry, of course, which gave no trouble at all. I can remember Miss Wardley, with her squeaking chalk, scrawling the blackboard like a shopping list:

'Write a poem—which *must* scan—on one or more of the following; A Kitten. Fairies. My Holidays. An Old Tinker. Charity. Sea Wrack . . .' ('What's that, miss?')

But it was easy in those days, one wrote a dozen an hour, one simply didn't hesitate, just began at the beginning and worked steadily through the subjects, ticking them off with indefatigible rhymes.

Sometimes there was a beating, which nobody minded—except an occasional red-faced mother. Sometimes a man came and took out our teeth. ('My mum says you ain't to take out any double-'uns . . .' '. . . Fourteen, fifteen, sixteen, seventeen . . .' 'Is they all double-'uns?' 'Shut up, you little horror.') Sometimes the Squire would pay us a visit, hand out prizes and make a misty-eyed speech. Sometimes an Inspector arrived on a bicycle and counted our heads and departed. Meanwhile Miss Wardley moved jingling amongst us, instructing, appealing, despairing:

'You're a grub, Walter Kerry. You have the wits of a hen. You're a great hulking lout of an oaf. You can just stay behind and do it over again. You can all stay behind, the lot of you.'

When lessons grew too tiresome, or too insoluble, we had our traditional ways of avoiding them.

'Please, miss, I got to stay 'ome tomorrow, to 'elp with the washing—the pigs—me dad's sick.'

'I dunno, miss; you never learned us that.'

'I 'ad me book stole, miss. Carry Burdock pinched it.'

'Please, miss, I got a gurt 'eadache.'

Sometimes these worked, sometimes they didn't. But once, when some tests hung over our heads, a group of us boys evaded them entirely by stinging our hands with horseflies. The task took all day, but the results were spectacular—our hands swelled like elephants' trunks. 'T'was a swarm, please, miss. They set on us. We run, by they stung us awful.' I remember how we groaned, and that we couldn't hold our pens, but I don't remember the pain.

At other times, of course, we forged notes from our mothers, or made ourselves sick with berries, or claimed to be relations of the corpse at funerals (the churchyard lay only next door). It was easy to start wailing when the hearse passed by, 'It's my auntie, miss—it's my cousin Wilf—can I go miss, please miss, can I?' Many a lone coffin was followed to its grave by a straggle of long-faced children, pinched, solemn, raggedly dressed, all strangers to the astonished bereaved.

So our school work was done—or where would we be today? We would be as we are; watching a loom or driving a tractor, and counting in images of fives and tens. This was as much as we seemed to need, and Miss Wardley did not add to the burden. What we learned in her care were the less formal truths—the names of flowers, the habits of birds, the intimacy of objects in being set to draw them, the treacherous innocence of boys, the sly charm of girls, the idiot's soaring fancies, and the tongue-tied dunce's informed authority when it came to talking about stoats. We were as merciless and cruel as most primitives are. But we learnt at that school the private nature of cruelty; and our inborn hatred for freaks and outcasts was tempered by meeting them daily.

There was Nick and Edna from up near the

Cross, the children of that brother and sister—the boy was strong and the girl was beautiful, and it was not at school that we learned to condemn them. And there was the gypsy boy Rosso, who lived up the quarry where his tribe had encamped for the summer. He had a chocolate-smooth face and crisp black curls, and at first we cold-shouldered him. He was a real outsider (they ate snails, it was said) and his slant Indian eyes repelled us. Then one day, out of hunger, he stole some sandwiches and was given the cane by Miss Wardley. Whatever the rights and wrongs of the case, that made him one of us.

We saw him run out of school, grizzling from the beating, and kneel down to tie up his boots. The shopkeeper's wife, passing by at that moment, stopped to preach him a little sermon. 'You didn't have to steal, even if you was that hungry. Why didn't you come to me?' The boy gave her a look, picked himself up, and ran off without a word. He knew, as we did, the answer to that one: we set our dogs on the gypsies here. As we walked back home to our cabbage dinners we were all of us filled with compassion. We pictured poor Rosso climbing back to his quarry, hungry to his miserable tents, with nothing but mud and

70

puddles to sit in and the sour banks to scavenge for food. Gypsies no longer seemed either sinister or strange. No wonder they eat snails, we thought.

★   ★   ★

The narrow school was just a conveyor belt along which the short years drew us. We entered the door marked 'Infants', moved gradually to the other, and were then handed back to the world. Lucky, lucky point of time; our eyes were on it always. Meanwhile we had moved to grander desks, saw our juniors multiplying in number, Miss Wardley suddenly began to ask our advice and to spoil us as though we were dying. There was no more to be done, no more to be learned. We began to look round the schoolroom with nostalgia and impatience. During playtime in the road we walked about gravely, patronizing the younger creatures. No longer the trembling, white-faced battles, the flights, the buttering-up of bullies; just a punch here and there to show our authority, then a sober stroll with our peers.

At last Miss Wardley was wringing our hands, tender and deferential. 'Good-bye, old chaps, and jolly good luck! Don't forget to

71

come back and see me.' She gave each one of us a coy sad glance. She knew that we never would.

THE KITCHEN

OUR house, and our life in it, is something of
which I still constantly dream, helplessly
bidden, night after night, to return to its tranquillity and nightmares: to the heavy shadows
of its stone-walled rooms creviced between
bank and yew trees, to its boarded ceilings
and gaping mattresses, its blood-shot geranium windows, its smells of damp pepper and
mushroom growths, its chaos, and rule of
women.

We boys never knew any male authority.
My father left us when I was three, and apart
from some rare and fugitive visits he did not
live with us again. He was a knowing, brisk,
elusive man, the son and the grandson of sai-
lors, but having himself no stomach for the
sea he had determined to make good on land.
In his miniature way he succeeded in this. He
became, while still in his middle teens, a
grocer's assistant, a local church organist, an
expert photographer and a dandy. Certain
portraits he took of himself at that time show
a handsome though threadbare lad, tall and
slender, and much addicted to gloves, high-
collars and courtly poses. He was clearly a cut

above the average, in charm as well as ambition. By the age of twenty he had married the beautiful daughter of a local merchant, and she bore him eight children—of whom five survived—before dying herself still young. Then he married his housekeeper, who bore him four more, three surviving, of which I was one. At the time of this second marriage he was still a grocer's assistant, and earning nineteen shillings a week. But his dearest wish was to become a Civil Servant, and he studied each night to this end. The First World War gave him the chance he wanted, and though properly distrustful of arms and battle he instantly sacrificed both himself and his family, applied for a post in the Army Pay Corps, went off to Greenwich in a bullet-proof vest and never permanently lived with us again.

He was a natural fixer, my father was, and things worked out pretty smoothly. He survived his clerk-stool war with a War Office pension (for nervous rash, I believe), then entered the Civil Service, as he had planned to do, and settled in London for good. Thus enabling my Mother to raise both his families, which she did out of love and pity, out of unreasoning loyalty and a fixed belief that he would one day return to her. . . .

74

*   *   *

Meanwhile, we lived where he had left us; a relic of his provincial youth; a sprawling, cumbersome, countrified brood too incongruous to carry with him. He sent us money, and we grew up without him; and I, for one, scarcely missed him. I was perfectly content in this world of women, muddle-headed though it might be, to be bullied and tumbled through the hand-to-mouth days, patched or dressed-up, scolded, admired, swept off my feet in sudden passions of kisses, or dumped forgotten among the unwashed pots.

My three half-sisters shared much of Mother's burden, and were the good fortune of our lives. Generous, indulgent, warm-blooded and dotty, these girls were not hard to admire. They seemed wrapped as it were in a perpetual bloom, the glamour of their grown-up teens, and expressed for us boys all that women should be in beauty, style and artifice.

For there was no doubt at all about their beauty, or the naturalness with which they wore it. Marjorie, the eldest, a blonde Aphrodite, appeared quite unconscious of the rarity of herself, moving always to measures

75

of oblivious grace and wearing her beauty like a kind of sleep. She was tall, long-haired and dreamily gentle, and her voice was low and slow. I never knew her to lose her temper, or to claim any personal justice. But I knew her to weep, usually for others, quietly, with large blue tears. She was a natural mother, and skilled with her needle, making clothes for us all when needed. With her constant beauty and balanced nature she was the tranquil night-light of our fears, a steady flame reassuring always, whose very shadows seemed thrown for our comfort.

Dorothy, the next one, was a wispy imp, pretty and perilous as a firework. Compounded equally of curiosity and cheek, a spark and tinder for boys, her quick dark body seemed writ with warnings that her admirers did well to observe. 'Not to be held in the hand,' it said. 'Light the touch-paper, but retire immediately.' She was an active forager who lived on thrills, provoked adventure and brought home gossip. Marjorie's were the ears to which most of it came, making her pause in her sewing, open wide her eyes and shake her head at each new revelation. 'You don't mean it, Doth! He *never*! NO! . . .' was all I seemed ever to hear.

Dorothy was as agile as a jungle cat, quicklimbed, entrancing, noisy. And she protected us boys with fire and spirit, and brought us treasures from the outside world. When I think of her now she is a coil of smoke, a giggling splutter, a reek of cordite. In repose she was also something else: a fairy-tale girl, blue as a plum, tender and sentimental.

The youngest of the three was cool, quiet Phyllis, a tobacco-haired, fragile girl, who carried her good looks with an air of apology, being the junior and somewhat shadowed. Marjorie and Dorothy shared a natural intimacy, being closer together in age, so Phyllis was the odd one, an unclassified solitary, compelled to her own devices. This she endured with a modest simplicity, quick to admire and slow to complain. Her favourite chore was putting us boys to bed, when she emerged in a strange light of her own, revealing a devout almost old-fashioned watchfulness, and gravely singing us to sleep with hymns.

Sad Phyllis, lit by a summer night, her tangled hair aglow, quietly sitting beside our beds, hands folded, eyes far away, singing and singing of 'Happy Eden' alone with her care over us—how often to this did I drop into sleep, feel the warmth of its tide engulf me, steered by her young hoarse hymning voice and tuneless reveries. . . .

These half-sisters I cherished; and apart from them I had two half-brothers also. Reggie, the first-born, lived apart with his grandmother; but young Harold, he lived with us. Harold was handsome, bony and secretive, and he loved our absent father. He stood somewhat apart, laughed down his nose, and was unhappy more often than not. Though younger than the girls, he seemed a generation older, was clever with his hands, but lost.

My own true brothers were Jack and Tony, and we three came at the end of the line. We were of Dad's second marriage, before he flew, and were born within the space of four years. Jack was the eldest, Tony the youngest, and myself the protected centre. Jack was the sharp one, bright as a knife, and was also my close companion. We played together, fought and ratted, built a private structure around us, shared the same bed till I finally left home, and lived off each other's brains. Tony, the baby—strange and beautiful waif—was a brooding, imaginative solitary. Like Phyllis he suffered from being the odd one of three; worse still, he was the odd one of seven. He was always either running to keep up with the rest of us sitting alone in the mud. His curious, crooked, suffering face had at times the radiance of a saint, at others the blank watchfulness of an insect. He could walk by himself or keep very still, get lost or appear at wrong moments. He drew like an artist, wouldn't read or write, swallowed beads by the boxful, sang and danced, was quite without fear, had secret friends, and was prey to terrible nightmares. Tony was the one true visionary amongst us, the tiny hermit no one quite understood. . . .

* * *

With our Mother, then, we made eight in that cottage and disposed of its three large floors. There was the huge white attic which ran the length of the house, where the girls slept on fat striped mattresses; an ancient, plaster-crumbling room whose sloping ceilings bulged like tentcloths. The roof was so thin that rain and bats filtered through, and you could hear a bird land on the tiles. Mother and Tony shared a bedroom below; Jack, Harold and I the other. But the house, since its building, had been so patched and parcelled that it was now almost impossible to get to one's room without first passing through someone else's. So each night saw a procession of pallid ghosts, sleepily seeking their beds, till the candle-snuffed darkness laid us out in rows, filed away in our allotted sheets, while snores and whistles shook the old house like a roundabout getting up steam.

But our waking life, and our growing years, were for the most part spent in the kitchen, and until we married, or ran away, it was the common room we shared. Here we lived and fed in a family fug, not minding the little space, trod on each other like birds in a hole, elbowed our ways without spite, all talking at once or all silent at once, or crying against each other, but never I think feeling overcrowded, being as separate as notes in a scale.

That kitchen, worn by our boots and lives, was scruffy, warm and low, whose fuss of furniture seemed never the same but was shuffled around each day. A black grate crackled with coal and beech-twigs; towels toasted on the guard; the mantel was littered with fine old china, horse brasses and freak potatoes. On the floor were strips of muddy matting, the windows were choked with plants, the walls supported stopped clocks and calendars, and smoky fungus ran over the ceilings. There were also six tables of different sizes, some armchairs gapingly stuffed, boxes, stools and unravelling baskets, books and papers on every chair, a sofa for cats, a harmonium for coats, and a piano for dust and photographs. These were the shapes of our kitchen landscape, the rocks of our submarine life, each object worn smooth by our constant nuzzling, or encrusted by lively barnacles, relics of birthdays and dead relations, wrecks of furniture long since foundered, all silted deep by mother's newspapers which the years piled round on the floor.

*   *   *

Waking up in the morning I saw squirrels in the yew trees nibbling at the moist red berries. Between the trees and the window hung a cloud of gold air composed of floating seeds and spiders. Farmers called to their cows on the other side of the valley and moorhens piped from the ponds. Brother Jack, as always, was the first to move, while I pulled on my boots in bed. We both stood at last on the bare-wood floor, scratching and saying our prayers. Too stiff and manly to say them out loud, we stood back to back and muttered them, and if an audible plea should slip out by chance, one just burst into song to cover it.

81

Singing and whistling were useful face-savers, especially when confounded by argument. We used the trick readily, one might say monotonously, and this morning it was Jack who began it.

'What's the name of the king, then?' he said, groping for his trousers.

'Albert.'

'No, it's not. It's George.'

'That's what I said you, didn't I? George.'

'No you never. You don't know. You're feeble.'

'Not so feeble as you be, any road.'

'You're balmy. You got brains of a bed-bug.'

'Da-da-di-da-da.'

'I said you're brainless. You can't even count.'

'Turrelee-turrelie. . . . Didn't hear you.'

'Yes you did then, blockhead. Fat and lazy. Big faa—'

'Dum-di-dah! . . . Can't hear. . . . Hey nonnie! . . .'

Well, that was all right; honours even, as usual. We broke the sleep from our eyes and dressed quickly.

Walking downstairs there was a smell of floorboards, of rags, sour lemons, old spices.

The smoky kitchen was in its morning muddle, from which breakfast would presently emerge. Mother stirred the porridge in a soot-black pot. Tony was carving bread with a ruler, the girls in their mackintoshes were laying the table, and the cats were eating the butter. I cleaned some boots and pumped up some fresh water; Jack went for a jug of skimmed milk.

'I'm all behind,' Mother said to the fire. 'This wretched coal's all slack.'

She snatched up an oil-can and threw it all on the fire. A belch of flame roared up the chimney. Mother gave a loud scream, as she always did, and went on stirring the porridge.

'If I had a proper stove,' she said. 'It's a trial getting you off each day.'

I sprinkled some sugar on a slice of bread and bolted it down while I could. How different again looked the kitchen this morning, swirling with smoke and sunlight. Some cut-glass vases threw jagged rainbows across the piano's field of dust, while Father in his pince-nez up on the wall looked down like a scandalized god.

At last the porridge was dabbed on our plates from a thick and steaming spoon. I covered the smoky lumps with treacle and began to eat from the sides to the middle. The

83

girls round the table chewed moonishly, wrapped in their morning stupor. Still sick with sleep, their mouths moved slow, hung slack while their spoon came up; then they paused for a moment, spoon to lip, collected their wits, and ate. Their vacant eyes stared straight before them, glazed at the sight of the day. Pink and glowing from their dreamy beds, from who knows what arms of heroes, they seemed like mute spirits hauled back to the earth after paradise feasts of love.

'Golly!' cried Doth. 'Have you seen the time?'

They began to jump to their feet.

'Goodness, it's late.'

'I got to be off.'

'Me too.'

'Lord, where's my things?'

'Well, ta-ta Ma; ta boys—be good.'

'Anything you want up from the Stores . . .?'

They hitched up their stockings, patted their hats and went running up the bank. This was the hour when walkers and bicyclists flowed down the long hills to Stroud, when the hooters called through the morning dews and factories puffed out their plumes. From each crooked corner of Stroud's five valleys girls were running to shops and looms,

84

with sleep in their eyes, and eggy cheeks, and in their ears night voices fading. Marjorie was off to her Milliner's Store, Phyllis to her Boots-and-Shoes, Dorothy to her job as junior clerk in a decayed cloth-mill by a stream. As for Harold, he'd started work already, his day began at six, when he'd leave the house with an angry shout for the lathe-work he really loved.

But what should we boys do, now they had all gone? If it was school-time, we pushed off next. If not, we dodged up the bank to play, ran snail races along the walls, or dug in the garden and found potatoes and cooked them in tins on the rubbish heap. We were always hungry, always calling for food, always seeking it in cupboards and hedges. But holiday mornings were a time of risk, there might be housework or errands to do. Mother would be ironing, or tidying-up, or reading books on the floor. So if we hung round the yard we kept our ears cocked; if she caught us, the game was up.

'Ah, there you are, son. I'm needing some salt. Pop to Vick's for a lump, there's a dear.'

Or: 'See if Granny Trill's got a screw of tea—only ask her nicely, mind.'

Or: 'Run up to Miss Turk and try and borrow half-crown; I didn't know I'd got so low.'

'Ask our Jack, our mother! I borrowed the bacon. It's blummin'-well his turn now.'

But Jack had slid off like an eel through the grass, making his sly get-away as usual. He was jumpy, shifty and quick-off-the-mark, an electric flex of nerves, skinny compared with the rest of us, or what farmers might call a 'poor doer'. If they had, in fact, they would have been quite wrong, for Jack did himself very well. He had developed a mealtime strategy which ensured that he ate for two. Speed and guile were the keys to his success, and we hungry ones called him The Slider.

Jack ate against time, that was really his secret; and in our house you had to do it. Imagine us all sitting down to dinner; eight round a pot of stew. It was lentil-stew usually, a heavy brown mash made apparently of plastic studs. Though it smelt of hot stables, we were used to it, and it was filling enough—could you get it. But the size of our family outstripped the size of the pot, so there was never quite enough to go round.

When it came to serving, Mother had no method, not even the law of chance—a dab on each plate in any old order and then every man for himself. No grace, no warning, no starting-gun; but the first to finish what he'd had on his plate could claim what was left in

86

the pot. Mother's swooping spoon was breathlessly watched—let the lentils fall where they may. But starveling Jack had worked it all out, he followed the spoon with his plate. Absentmindedly Mother would give him first dollop, and very often a second, and as soon as he got it swallowed it whole, not using his teeth at all. 'More please, I've finished'—the bare plate proved it, so he got the pot-scrapings too. Many's the race I've lost to him thus, being just that second slower. But it left me marked with an ugly scar, a twisted, food-crazed nature, so that still I am calling for whole rice puddings and big pots of stew in the night.

*   *   *

The day was over and we had used it, running errands or prowling the fields. When evening came we returned to the kitchen, back to its smoky comfort, in from the rapidly cooling air to its wrappings of warmth and cooking. We boys came first, scuffling down the bank, singly, like homing crows. Long tongues of shadows licked the curves of the fields and the trees turned plump and still. I had been off to Painswick to pay the rates, running fast through the long wet grass, and now I was back, panting hard, the job finished, with hay seeds stuck to my legs. A plate of blue smoke hung above our chimney, flat in the motionless air, and every stone in the path as I ran down home shook my bones with arriving joy.

We chopped wood for the night and carried it in; dry beech sticks as brittle as candy. The baker came down with a basket of bread slung carelessly over his shoulder. Eight quartern loaves, cottage-size, black-crusted, were handed in at the door. A few crisp flakes of pungent crust still clung to his empty basket, so we scooped them up on our spit-wet fingers and laid them upon our tongues. The twilight gathered, the baker shouted good-night, and whistled his way up the bank. Up in the road his black horse waited, the cart lamps smoking red.

Indoors, our Mother was cooking pancakes, her face aglow from the fire. There was a smell of sharp lemon and salty batter, and a burning hiss of oil. The kitchen was dark and convulsive with shadows, no light had yet been lit. Flames leapt, subsided, corners woke and died, fires burned in a thousand brasses.

'Poke round for the matches, dear boy,' said Mother. 'Damn me if I know where they got to.'

We lit the candles and set them about, each in its proper order: two on the mantelpiece, one on the piano, and one on a plate in the window. Each candle suspended a ball of light, a luminous fragile glow, which swelled and contracted to the spluttering wick or leaned to the moving air. Their flames pushed weakly against the red of the fire, too tenuous to make much headway, revealing our faces more by casts of darkness than by any clear light they threw.

Next we filled and lit the tall iron lamp and placed it on the table. When the wick had warmed and was drawing properly, we turned it up full strength. The flame in the funnel then sprang alive and rose like a pointed flower, began to sing and shudder and grow more radiant, throwing pools of light on the ceiling. Even so, the kitchen remained mostly in shadow, its walls a voluptuous gloom.

The time had come for my violin practice. I began twanging the strings with relish. Mother was still frying and rolling up pancakes; my brothers lowered their heads and sighed. I propped my music on the mantelpiece and sliced through a Russian Dance while sweet smells of resin mixed with lemon and fat as the dust flew in clouds from my bow. Now and then I got a note just right, and then

Mother would throw me a glance. A glance of piercing, anxious encouragement as she side-stepped my swinging arm. Plump in her slippers, one hand to her cheek, her pan beating time in the other, her hair falling down about her ears, mouth working to help out the tune—old and tired though she was, her eyes were a girl's, and it was for looks such as these that I played.

'Splendid!' she cried. 'Top-hole! Clap-clap! Now give us another, me lad.'

So I slashed away at 'William Tell', and when I did that, plates jumped; and Mother skipped gaily around the hearth-rug, and even Tony rocked a bit in his chair.

Meanwhile Jack had cleared some boots from the table and started his inscrutable homework. Tony, in his corner, began to talk to the cat and play with some fragments of cloth. So with the curtains drawn close and the pancakes coming, we settled down to the evening. When the kettle boiled and the toast was made, we gathered and had our tea. We grabbed and dodged and passed and snatched, and packed our mouths like pelicans.

Mother ate always standing up, tearing crusts off the loaf with her fingers, a hand-to-mouth feeding that expressed her vigilance, like that of a wireless-operator at sea. For most of Mother's attention was fixed on the grate, whose fire must never go out. When it threatened to do so she became seized with hysteria, wailing and wringing her hands, pouring on oil and chopping up chairs in a frenzy to keep it alive. In fact it seldom went out completely, though it was very often ill. But Mother nursed it with skill, banking it up every night and blowing hard on the bars every morning. The state of our fire became as important to us as it must have been to a primitive tribe. When it sulked and sank we were filled with dismay; when it blazed all was well with the world; but if—God save us—it went out altogether, then we were clutched by primeval chills. Then it seemed that the very sun had died, that winter had come for ever, that the wolves of the wilderness were gathering near, and that there was no more hope to look for. . . .

But tonight the firelight snapped and crackled, and Mother was in full control. She ruled the range and all its equipment with a tireless, nervous touch. Eating with one hand, she threw on wood with the other, raked the ashes and heated the oven, put on a kettle, stirred the pot, and spread out some more shirts on the guard. As soon as we boys had finished our tea, we pushed all the crockery aside, piled it up roughly at the far end of the table, and settled down under the lamp. Its light was warm and live around us, a kind of puddle of fire of its own. I set up my book and began to draw. Jack worked at his notes and figures. Tony was playing with some cotton reels, pushing them slowly round the table.

All was silent except for Tony's voice, softly muttering his cotton-reel story.

'. . . So they come out of this big hole see, and the big chap said Fie he said we'll kill 'em see, and the pirates was waiting up 'ere, and they had this gurt cannon and they went bang fire and the big chap fell down wheeee! and rolled back in the 'ole and I said we got 'em and I run up the 'ill and this boat see was comin' and I jumped on board wooosh cruump and I said now I'm captain see and they said fie and I took me 'achet' 'ack 'ack and they all fell plop in the sea wallop and I sailed the boat round 'ere and round 'ere and up 'ere and round 'ere and down 'ere and up 'ere and round 'ere and down 'ere . . .'

*   *   *

Now the girls arrived home in their belted mackintoshes, flushed from their walk through the dark, and we looked up from our games and said; 'Got anything for us?' and Dorothy gave us some liquorice. Then they all had their supper at one end of the table while we boys carried on at the other. When supper was over and cleared away, the kitchen fitted us all. We drew together round the evening lamp, the vast and easy time. . . . Marjorie began to trim a new hat, Dorothy to write a love-letter, Phyllis sat down with some forks and spoons, blew ah! and sleepily rubbed them. Harold, home late, cleaned his bike in a corner. Mother was cutting up newspapers.

We talked in spurts, in lowered voices, scarcely noticing if anyone answered.

'I turned a shaft to a thou' today,' said Harold.

'A what?'

'He said a "thou".'

Chairs creaked awhile as we thought about it. . . .

'Charlie Revell's got a brand new suit. He had it made to fit. . . .'

'He half fancies himself.'

'Charlie Revell! . . .'

Pause.

'Look, Doth, I got these bits for sixpence. I'm going to stitch 'em all round the top here.'

'Mmmmm. Well. Tccch-tcch. S'all

right. . . .'

'Dr Green came up to the shop this morning. Wearing corduroy bloomers. Laugh! . . .'

'Look, Ma, look! I've drawn a church on fire. Look, Marge, Doth! Hey, look! . . .'

'If x equals x, then y equals z—shut up!—if x is y . . .'

'O Madeline, if you'll be mine, I'll take you oe'r the sea, di-dah . . .'

'Look what I've cut for my scrapbook, girls—a Beefeater—isn't he killing?'

'Charlie Revell cheeked his dad today. He called him a dafty. He . . .'

'. . . You know that boy from the Dairy, Marge—the one they call Barnacle Boots? Well, he asked me to go to Spot's with him. I told him to run off home.'

'No! You never!'

'I certainly did. I said I don't go to no pictures with butter-wallopers. You should have seen his face. . . .'

'Harry Lazbury smells of chicken-gah. I had to move me desk.'

'Just hark who's talking. Dainty Dick.'

'I'll never be ready by Sunday. . . .'

'I've found a lovely snip for my animal page—an old seal—look girls, the expression! . . .'

'So I went round 'ere, and down round 'ere,

and he said fie so I went 'ack, 'ack . . .'

'What couldn't I do to a nice cream slice. . . .'

'Charlie Revell's had 'is ears syringed. . . .'

'D'you remember, Doth, when we went to Spots, and they said Children in Arms Not Allowed, and we walked little Tone right up the steps and he wasn't even two. . . .'

Marge gave her silky, remembering laugh and looked fondly across at Tony. The fire burned clear with a bottle-green light. Their voices grew low and furry. A farm-dog barked far across the valley, fixing the time and distance exactly. Warned by the dog and some hooting owls, I could sense the night valley emptying, stretching in mists of stars and water, growing slowly more secret and late.

The kitchen, warm and murmuring now, vibrated with rosy darkness. My pencil began to wander on the page, my eyes to cloud and clear. I thought I'd stretch myself out on the sofa—for a while, for a short while only. The girls' muted chatter went on and on; I struggled to catch the drift. 'Sh! . . . Not now. . . . When the boys are in bed. . . . You'll die when you hear. . . . Not now. . . .'

The boards on the ceiling were melting like water. Words broke and went floating away. Chords of smooth music surged up in my

95

head, thick tides of warmth overwhelmed me, I was drowning in langours of feathered seas, spiralling cosily down. . . .

Once in a while I was gently roused to a sound amplified by sleep; to the fall of a coal, the sneeze of the cat, or a muted exclamation. 'She couldn't have done such a thing. . . . She did. . . .' 'Done what? . . . What thing? Tell, tell me. . . .' But helpless I glided back to sleep, deep in the creviced seas, the blind waters stilled me, weighed me down, the girls' words floated on top. I lay longer now, and deeper far; heavier weeds were falling on me. . . .

'Come on, Loll. Time to go to bed. They boys went up long ago.' The whispering girls bent over me; the kitchen returned upside down. 'Wake up, lamb. . . . He's wacked to the wide. Let's try and carry him up.'

Half-waking, half-carried, they got me up-stairs. I felt drunk and tattered with dreams. They dragged me stumbling round the bend in the landing, and then I smelt the sweet blankets of bed.

It was cold in the bedroom; there were no fires here. Jack lay open-mouthed, asleep. Shivering, I swayed while the girls undressed me, giggling around my buttons. They left me my shirt and my woollen socks, then stuffed

96

me between the sheets.

Away went the candle down the stairs, boards creaked and the kitchen door shut. Darkness. Shapes returning slow. The window a square of silver. My bed-half was cold—Jack hot as a bird. For a while I lay doubled, teeth-chattering, blowing, warming against him slowly.

'Keep yer knees to yerself,' said Jack, turning over. He woke. 'Say, think of a number!'

' 'Leven-hundered and two,' I groaned, in a trance.

'Double it,' he hissed in my ear.

Double it. . . . Twenny-four hundred and what? Can't do it. Something or other. . . . A dog barked again and swallowed a goose. The kitchen still murmured downstairs. Jack quickly submerged, having fired off his guns, and began snorkling away at my side. Gradually I straightened my rigid limbs and hooked all my fingers together. I felt wide awake now. I thought I'd count to a million. 'One, two . . .' I said; that's all.

GRANNIES IN THE
WAINSCOT

OUR house was seventeenth-century Cotswold, and was handsome as they go. It was
built of stone, had hand-carved windows,
golden surfaces, moss-flaked tiles, and walls
so thick they kept a damp chill inside them
whatever the season or weather. Its attics and
passages were full of walled-up doors which
our fingers longed to open—doors that led to
certain echoing chambers now sealed off from
us for ever. The place had once been a small
country manor, and later a public beerhouse;
but it had decayed even further by the time we
got to it, and was now three poor cottages in
one. The house was shaped like a T, and we
lived in the down-stroke. The top-stroke—
which bore into the side of the bank like a
rusty expended shell—was divided separately
among two old ladies, one's portion lying
above the other's.

Granny Trill and Granny Wallon were
rival ancients and lived on each other's
nerves, and their perpetual enmity was like
mice in the walls and absorbed much of my
early days. With their sickle-bent bodies, pale

98

pink eyes, and wild wisps of hedgerow hair, they looked to me the very images of witches and they were also much alike. In all their time as such close neighbours they never exchanged a word. They communicated instead by means of boots and brooms— jumping on floors and knocking on ceilings. They referred to each other as 'Er-Down-Under' and 'Er-Up-Atop, the Varmint'; for each to the other was an airy nothing, a local habitation not fit to be named.

'Er-Down-Under, who lived on our level, was perhaps the smaller of the two, a tiny white shrew who came nibbling through her garden, who clawed squeaking with gossip at our kitchen window, or sat sucking bread in the sun; always mysterious and self-contained and feather-soft in her movements. She had two names, which she changed at will according to the mood of her day. Granny Wallon was her best, and stemmed, we were told, from some distinguished alliance of the past. Behind this crisp and trotting body were certainly rumours of noble blood. But she never spoke of them herself. She was known to have raised a score of children. And she was known to be very poor. She lived on cabbage, bread and potatoes—but she also made excellent wines.

Granny Wallon's wines were famous in the village, and she spent a large part of her year preparing them. The gathering of the ingredients was the first of the mysteries. At the beginning of April she would go off with her baskets and work round the fields and hedges, and every fine day till the end of summer would find her somewhere out in the valley. One saw her come hobbling home in the evening, bearing her cargoes of crusted flowers, till she had buckets of cowslips, dandelions, elder-blossom crammed into every corner of the house. The elder-flower, drying on her kitchen floor, seemed to cover it with a rancid carpet, a crumbling rime of grey-green blossom fading fast in a dust of summer. Later the tiny grape-cluster of the elderberry itself would be seething in purple vats, with daisies and orchids thrown in to join it, even strands of the dog-rose bush.

What seasons fermented in Granny Wallon's kitchen, what summers were brought to the boil, with limp flower-heads piled around the floor holding fast to their clotted juices—the sharp spiced honey of those cowslips first, then the coppery reeking dandelion, the bitter poppy's whiff of powder, the cat's-breath, death-green elder. Gleanings of days and a dozen pastures, strippings of lanes and hedges—she bore them home to her flag-tiled kitchen, sorted them each from each, built up her fires and loaded her pots, and added her sugar and yeast. The vats boiled daily in suds of sugar, revolving petals in throbbing water, while the air aromatic, steamy, embalmed, distilled the hot dews and flowery soups and ran the wine down the dripping walls.

And not only flower-heads went into these brews; the old lady used parsnips, too, potatoes, sloes, crab-apples, quinces, in fact anything she could lay her hands on. Granny Wallon made wine as though demented, out of anything at all; and no doubt, if given enough sugar and yeast, could have made a drink out of a box of old matches.

She never hurried or hoarded her wines, but led them gently through their natural stages. After the boiling they were allowed to settle and to work in the cool of the vats. For several months, using pieces of toast, she scooped off their yeasty sediments. Then she bottled and labelled each liquor in turn and put them away for a year.

At last one was ready, then came the day of distribution. A squeak and a rattle would shake our window, and we'd see the old lady, wispily grinning, waving a large white jug in

101

her hand.

'Hey there, missus! Try this'n, then. It's the first of my last year's cowslip.'

Through the kitchen window she'd fill up our cups and watch us, head cocked, while we drank. The wine in the cups was still and golden, transparent as a pale spring morning. It smelt of ripe grass in some far-away field and its taste was as delicate as air. It seemed so innocent, we would swig away happily and even the youngest guzzled it down. Then a curious rocking would seize the head; tides rose from our feet like a fever, the kitchen walls began to shudder and shift, and we all fell in love with each other.

Very soon we'd be wedged, tight-crammed, in the window, waving our cups for more, while our Mother, bright-eyed, would be mumbling gaily:

'Lord bless you, Granny. Fancy cowsnips and parsney. You must give me the receipt, my dear.'

Granny Wallon would empty the jug in our cups, shake out the last drops on the flowers, then trot off tittering down the garden path, leaving us hugging ourselves in the window.

*   *   *

Whatever the small indulgences with which Granny Wallon warmed up her old life, her neighbour, Granny Trill, had none of them. For Er-Up-Atop was as frugal as a sparrow and as simple in her ways as a grub. She could sit in her chair for hours without moving, a veil of blackness over her eyes, a suspension like frost on her brittle limbs, with little to show that she lived at all save the gentle motion of her jaws. One of the first things I noticed about old Granny Trill was that she always seemed to be chewing, sliding her folded gums together in a daylong ruminative cud. I took this to be one of the tricks of age, a kind of slowed-up but protracted feasting. I imagined her being delivered a quartern loaf—say, on a Friday night—then packing the lot into her rubbery cheeks and chewing them slowly through the week. In fact, she never ate bread at all—or butter, or meat, or vegetables—she lived entirely on tea and biscuits, and on porridge sent up by the Squire.

Granny Trill had an original sense of time which seemed to obey some vestigial pattern. She breakfasted, for instance, at four in the morning, had dinner at ten, took tea at two-thirty, and was back in her bed at five. This régime never varied either winter or summer, and belonged very likely to her childhood days when she lived in the woods with her father. To me it seemed a monstrous arrangement, upsetting the roots of order. But Granny Trill's time was for God, or the birds, and although she had a clock she kept it simply for the tick, its hands having dropped off years ago.

In contrast to the subterranean, almost cavernous life which Granny Wallon lived down under, Granny Trill's cottage door was always open and her living-room welcomed us daily. Not that she could have avoided us anyway, for she lay at our nimble mercy. Her cottage was just outside our gate and there were geraniums in pots round the door. Her tiny room opened straight on to the bank and was as visible as a last year's bird's-nest. Smells of dry linen and tea-caddies filled it, together with the sweeter tang of old flesh.

'You at home, Granny Trill? You in there, Gran?'

Of course—where else would she be? We heard her creaking sigh from within.

'Well, I'll be bound. That you varmints again?'

'We come on a visit, Gran.'

'Just mind them pots then, or I'll cut you to pieces.'

The three of us clumped indoors. Granny

Trill was perched in the windowsill, combing her thin white hair.

'What you doing, Gran?'

'Just biding still. Just biding and combing me bits.'

The room was blue and hazy with wood-smoke. We prowled slowly around its treasures, opening boxes, filling tea-pots with cotton-reels, skimming plates along the floor. The old lady sat and watched us mildly, taking very little notice, while her dry yellow arm swept up and down, and the black-toothed comb, as it slid through her hair, seemed to be raking the last ash of a fire.

'You going bald, Gran?'

'I still got me bits.'

'It's coming out.'

'No, it ain't.'

'Look at that dead stuff dropping out of yer comb.'

'That's healthy. It makes room for more.'

We didn't think it mattered; it was merely conversation, any subject at all would do. But suddenly the old lady skipped out of her seat and began to leap up and down on the floor.

' 'Er down there! I got more than 'er! 'Er's bald as a tater root! Wicked old lump, I'll see 'er gone. 'Er's failing, you mark my words.'

When the spasm was over, she was back in

the window, winding her hair into a fragile bun. Beautiful were the motions of her shrunken hands, their movements so long rehearsed; her fingers flew and coiled and pinned, worked blind without aid of a mirror. The result was a structure of tight perfection, a small shining ball of snow.

'Get yer hands from me drawers! Them's female things!'

She sat relaxed now her hair was done, put on her cracked and steel-rimmed glasses, unhooked the almanac from the wall, and began to read bits out aloud. She read in a clear and solemn voice, as though from the Holy Writ.

'"Tragic Intelligence of a Disaster at Sea, in the Region of the Antipoods." That's for June, poor creatures, with their families an' all. "A Party of Scientists Will Slip Down a Crevice, With Certain Resultant Fatalities. . . ." Oh, dear, oh well, if they must poke round them places. "A Murdered Cadaver will be Shockingly Uncovered in a Western Industrial Town." There, what did I tell you! I knew that'd come. I been expecting that.' She began to skip pages, running through the months, but giving weight to the Warnings that struck her. '"Crisis in Parliament" . . . "House Struck by Fireball". . . . "Riots". . . .

106

"A Royal Surprise".... "Turkish Massacre".... "Famine".... "War".... "The King will Suffer a Slight Infirmity."...' The catalogue of disasters seemed to give her peace, to confirm her sense of order. In Old Moore's pages she saw the future's worst, saw it and was not dismayed. Such alarms were neither threats nor prophecies but simply repetitions; were comforting, frightful and familiar, being composed of all that had fashioned her long past, the poisoned cuds she had so patiently chewed, swallowed and yet survived.

'Ah, well,' she said placidly, as she lay down the book; 'He foresees some monstrous doings. A terrible year it looks to be. And he says we'll have hail on Tuesday....'

We boys took up the almanac and leafed through the pages, seeking the more ominous pictures. We saw drawings of skies cracked across by lightning, of church towers falling, multitudes drowning, of men in frockcoats shaking warning fingers, of coffins laden with crowns. The drawings were crude but jaggedly vital, like scratches on a prison wall. We relished them much as did Granny Trill, as signs of an apocalypse which could not touch us. In them we saw the whole outside world, split, convulsive and damned. It had nothing, of course, to do with our village; and we felt like gods, both compassionate and cruel, as we savoured these bloody visions.

Granny Trill used the almanac as an appetizer; now she shifted to her table for dinner. She sopped a few biscuits in a cup of cold tea and scooped the wet crumbs into her mouth, then began grinding away with such an effort of gums one would have thought she was cracking bones. She wore, as usual, her black net dress, but her bright old head rising out of it looked like a flame on a smoking lamp. Her brow was noble, her pink eyes glittered, her nose swooped down like a finger; only the lower part of her face was collapsed and rubbery, but then that did all the work.

'You a hundred yet, Granny?'

'Nigh on—nigh on.'

'Have you got a dad?'

'Bless you, no; he died long since. He was killed by a tree over Ashcomb.'

She often told us the story of this, and now she told us again. Her father had been a woodcutter, strong as a giant—he could lift up a horse and wagon. From the age of five, when she lost her mother, she lived with him in the woods. They used to sleep in a tent, or a kind of wigwam of pine branches, and while her father was tree-felling, the little girl made

108

baskets and sold them around the village. For ten years they lived this life together and were perfectly contented. She grew up into a beautiful young girl—'Some'ow I seemed to send men breathless'—but her father was careful, and when the timber-men came he used to hide her under piles of sacking.

Then one day—she was fifteen years old at the time—a tree fell on her father. She heard him shout and ran up the thicket and found him skewered into the ground with a branch. He was lying face down and couldn't see her. 'I'm going, Alice,' he'd said. She clawed a hole with her hands and lay down beside him, and held him until he died. It took twenty-four hours, and she never moved, nor did he speak again.

When at last some carters discovered them, she was still lying with the body. She watched them roll the tree off him, and straighten his limbs, then she ran up the Scrubs and hid. She hid for a week near some fox-holes there, and neither ate nor drank. Then the Squire sent out some men to look for her, and when they found her she fought like a savage. But they managed to carry her down to the Manor, where she was given a bath and a bed. 'That was the first bath I ever had,' said Granny. 'It took six of 'em to get me soaped.'

But they nursed her and pacified her, and gave her housework to do, and later married her to George Trill, the gardener. 'He were a good man, too—he settled me. I was about sixteen years at the time. He was much like me dad, only a good bit slower—and a lot older than I, of course.'

When she finished her story her chin was resting in her cup and her features were abstracted and bright. Sharp little veins crackled around her eyes, and her skull pushed hard through the skin. Could she ever have been that strapping Alice whom the carters had chased through the woods? a girl of sixteen whom men washed and married? the age of our sister Dorothy? . . .

'Me dad planted that tree,' she said absently, pointing out through the old cracked window.

The great beech filled at least half the sky and shook shadows all over the house. Its roots clutched the slope like a giant hand, holding the hill in place. Its trunk writhed with power, threw off veils of green dust, rose towering into the air, branched into a thousand shaded alleys, became a city for owls and squirrels. I had thought such trees to be as old as the earth, I never dreamed that a man could make them. Yet it was Granny Trill's dad who had planted this tree, had thrust in the seed with his finger. How old must he have been to leave such a mark? Think of Granny's age, and add his on top, and you were back at the beginning of the world.

'He were a young man then, a-course,' said Granny. 'He set it afore he got married.' She squinted up at the height of the tree, and sat there nodding gently, while a branch of green shadows, thrown by its leaves, moved softly across her face.

'I got to see to summat!' she said abruptly, slipping creakily down from her chair. She left us then, gathered up her skirts, and trotted lightly along to the wood. We saw her squatting among the undergrowth, bright-eyed, like a small black partridge. Old age might compel her to live in a house, but for comfort she still went to the woods.

*   *   *

Granny Trill and Granny Wallon were tra-ditional ancients of a kind we won't see today, the last of that dignity of grandmothers to whom age was its own embellishment. The grandmothers of those days dressed for the part in that curious but endearing uniform which is now known to us only through

111

music-hall. And our two old neighbours, when setting forth on errands, always prepared themselves scrupulously so. They wore high laced boots and long muslin dresses, beaded chokers and candlewick shawls, crowned by tall poke bonnets tied with trailing ribbons and smothered with inky sequins. They looked like starlings, flecked with jet, and they walked in a tinkle of darkness.

Those severe and similar old bodies enthralled me when they dressed that way. When I finally became King (I used to think) I would command a parade of grandmas, and drill them, and march them up and down—rank upon rank of hobbling boots, nodding bonnets, flying shawls, and furious, chewing faces. They would be gathered from all the towns and villages and brought to my palace in wagon-loads. No more than a monarch's whim, of course, like eating cocoa or drinking jellies; but far more spectacular any day than those usual trudging guardsmen.

In spite of their formal dressing-up, the two old ladies never went very far—now and again to church for the sermon, and to the village shop once a week. Granny Wallon went for her sugar and yeast; Granny Trill for her tuppence of snuff.

Snuff was Granny T's one horrible vice,

and she indulged it with no moderation. A fine brown dust coated all her clothes and she had nostrils like badger-holes. She kept her snuff in a small round box, made of tin and worn smooth as a pebble. She was continually tapping and snapping it open, pinching a nailful, gasping *Ah!*, flicking her fingers and wiping her eyes, and leaving on the air a faint dry cloud like an explosion of fungoid dust.

The snuff-box repelled and excited us boys and we opened its lid with awe, Reeking substance of the underworld, clay-brown dust of decay, of powdered flesh and crushed old bones, rust-scrapings and the rubbish of graves. How sharp and stinging was this fearful spice, eddying up from its box, animating the air with tingling fumes like a secret breath of witchery. Though we clawed and sniffed it we could not enjoy it, but neither could we leave it alone.

'You at me snuff agen, you boys? I'll skin yer bottoms, I will!'

We looked up guiltily, saw her cackling face, so took a big pinch between us. With choking tears and head-rocking convulsions we rolled across the floor. The old lady regarded us with pleasure; our paroxysms shook the house.

'That'll learn you, I reckon; you thieving

mites. Here, give it to me, I'll show 'ee.'

She took up the box and tapped the lid, then elegantly fed her nose. A shudder of ecstasy closed her eyes. She was borne very far away.

*   *   *

One morning our Mother was paring apples, so we boys settled down to the peelings. They lay in green coils upon the table, exuding their tart fresh odours. Slowly we chewed through the juicy ribbons, mumbling our jaws as we went.

'I'm old Granny Trill, a-eating her dinner,' said Jack, sucking peel through his gums. A great joke, this; we chewed and moaned, making much of the toothless labour.

'Don't mock,' said our Mother. 'The poor, poor soul—alone by herself all day.'

We glanced at our sisters to share our wit, but got no encouragement there. They were absorbed as usual in some freakish labour, stitching dead birds on canvas hats.

'The poor lone creature,' our Mother went on, lowering her voice out of charity. 'It's a sin and a shame!' She raised it again. 'That's what it is—a crime! You girls ought to pop up and pay her a visit. You know how she dotes on you all.'

Our sisters had reached the impressive stage; they talked careful and dressed in splendour—as fine, that is, as they were able to do with the remnants that fell to their hands. With a short length here, a bit of tulle there, a feather picked up at a sale, a hedgehog of needles, a mouthful of pins, a lot of measuring, snipping and arguing—it was remarkable what raiment they managed to conjure considering what little they had.

They were always willing to put on a show, so they accepted Mother's suggestion. They decided to deck themselves out in their best and to give Gran Trill a treat. The attics were ransacked, the cupboards breached, and very soon all was uproar. Quarrelling, snatching, but smoothly efficient, they speedily draped themselves; took a tucket in here, let a gusset out there, spliced a waist or strapped up a bodice; in no time at all they were like paradise birds, and off they minced to see the old lady.

Enthralled as ever by their patchwork glories, I followed them closely behind. Beautiful Marge led the way up the path and rapped elegantly on Granny's door. Meanwhile Doth and Phyl hitched their slipping girdles, pushed the bandeaux out of their eyes, stood hands on hips making light conversation—two jazz-debs bright in the sun.

For once Granny Trill seemed hard of hearing, though the girls had knocked three times. So with a charming shrug and a fastidious sigh Marge swung a great kick at the door.

'Who's that?' came a frightened yelp from within.

'It's only us,' trilled the girls.

They waltzed through the door, apparitions of rose, striking postures straight out of *Home Notes*. 'How do we look then, Gran?' asked Marjorie. 'This line is the mode, you know. We copied it out of that pattern book. It's the rage in Stroud, they say.'

Riffling their feathers, arching their necks, catching copy reflections in mirrors, they paraded the room, three leggy flamingoes, each lit by a golden down. To me they were something out of the sky, airborne visions of fairy light; and with all the enthusiasm they were capable of they gave the old lady the works. Yet all was clearly not going well. There was a definite chill in the air. . . .

Granny watched them awhile, then her jaws snapped shut; worse still, her gums stopped chewing. Then she clapped her hands with a terrible crack.

'You baggages! You jumped-up varmints! Be off or I'll fetch me broom!'

The girls retreated at the dainty double, surprised but in no way insulted. Their sense of fashion was unassailable, for were they not up with the times? How could the old girl know about belts and bandeaux?—after all, she was only a peasant. . . .

But later Gran Trill took our Mother aside and spoke grimly of her concern.

'You better watch them gels of yourn. They'll bring shame on us one of these days. Strutting and tennis-playing and aping the gentry—it's carnal and blasphemy. Just you watch 'em, missus; I don't like their doings. Humble gels got to remember their stations.'

Mother, I fancy, was half with her there; but she wouldn't have dreamed of interfering.

*   *   *

For several more years the lives of the two old ladies continued to revolve in intimate enmity around each other. Like cold twin stars, linked but divided, they survived by a mutual balance. Both of them reached back similarly in time, shared the same modes and habits, the same sense of feudal order, the same rampaging terrible God. They were far

117

more alike than unalike, and could not abide each other.

They arranged things therefore so that they never met. They used separate paths when they climbed the bank, they shopped on different days, they relieved themselves in different areas, and staggered their church-going hours. But each one knew always what the other was up to, and passionately disapproved. Granny Wallon worked at her flowering vats, boiling and blending her wines; or crawled through her cabbages; or tapped on our windows, gossiped, complained, or sang. Granny Trill continued to rise in the dark, comb her waxen hair, sit out in the wood, chew, sniff and suck up porridge, and study her almanac. Yet between them they sustained a mutual awareness based solely on ear and nostril. When Granny Wallon's wines boiled, Granny Trill had convulsions; when Granny Trill took snuff, Granny Wallon had strictures—and neither let the other forget it. So all day they listened, sniffed and pried, rapping on floors and ceilings, and prowled their rooms with hawking coughs, chivvying each other long-range. It was a tranquil, bitter-pleasant life, perfected by years of custom; and to me they both seemed everlasting, deathless crones of an eternal mythology; they had always been somewhere there in the wainscot and I could imagine no world without them.

Then one day, as Granny Trill was clambering out of her wood, she stumbled and broke her hip. She went to bed then for ever. She lay patient and yellow in a calico coat, her combed hair fine as a girl's. She accepted her doom without complaint, as though some giant authority—Squire, father, or God—had ordered her there to receive it.

'I knowed it was coming,' she told our Mother, 'after that visitation. I saw it last week sitting at the foot of me bed. Some person in white; I dunno . . .'

There was a sharp early rap on our window next morning. Granny Wallon was bobbing outside.

'Did you hear him, missus?' she asked knowingly. 'He been a-screeching around since midnight.' The death-bird was Granny Wallon's private pet and messenger, and she gave a skip as she told us about him. 'He called three-a-four times. Up in them yews. Her's going, you mark my words.'

And that day indeed Granny Trill died, whose bones were too old to mend. Like a delicate pale bubble, blown a little higher and further than the other girls of her generation,

119

she had floated just long enough for us to catch sight of her, had hovered for an instant before our eyes; and then had popped suddenly, and disappeared for ever, leaving nothing on the air but a faint-drying image and the tiniest cloud of snuff.

The little church was packed for her funeral, for the old lady had been a landmark. They carried her coffin along the edge of the wood and then drew it on a cart through the village. Granny Wallon, dressed in a shower of jets, followed some distance behind; and during the service she kept to the back of the church and everybody admired her.

All went well till the lowering of the coffin, when there was a sudden and distressing commotion. Granny Wallon, ribbons flying, her bonnet awry, fought her way to the side of the grave.

'It's a lie!' she screeched, pointing down at the coffin. 'That baggage were younger'n me! 95, she says!—ain't more'n 90, an' I gone on 92! It's a crime you letting 'er go to 'er Maker got up in such brazen lies! Dig up the old devil! Get 'er brass plate off! It's insulting the living church! . . .'

They carried her away, struggling and crying, kicking out with her steel-sprung boots. Her cries grew fainter and were soon obliterated by the sounds of the grave-diggers' spades. The clump of clay falling on Granny Trill's coffin sealed her with her inscription for ever; for no one knew the truth of her age, there was no one old enough to know.

Granny Wallon had triumphed, she had buried her rival; and now there was no more to do. From then on she faded and diminished daily, kept to her house and would not be seen. Sometimes we heard mysterious knocks in the night, rousing and summoning sounds. But the days were silent, no one walked in the garden, or came skipping to claw at our window. The wine fires sank and died in the kitchen, as did the sweet fires of obsession.

About two weeks later, of no special disease, Granny Wallon gave up in her sleep. She was found on her bed, dressed in bonnet and shawl, with her signalling broom in her hand. Her open eyes were fixed on the ceiling in a listening stare of death. There was nothing in fact to keep her alive; no cause, no bite, no fury. Er-Down-Under had joined Er-Up-Atop, having lived closer than anyone knew.

PUBLIC DEATH,
PRIVATE MURDER

SOON after the First World War a violent event took place in the village which drew us together in a web of silence and cut us off for a while almost entirely from the outside world. I was too young at the time to be surprised by it, but I knew those concerned and learned the whole story early. Though it was seldom discussed—and never with strangers—the facts of that night were familiar to us all, and common consent buried the thing down deep and raked out the tracks around it. So bloody, raw and sudden it was, it resembled an outbreak of family madness which we took pains to conceal, out of shame and pride, and for the sake of those infected.

The crime occurred a few days before Christmas, on a night of deep snow and homecoming; the time when the families called in their strays for an annual feast of goose. The night was as cold as Cotswold cold can be, with a wind coming straight from the Arctic. We children were in bed blowing hard on our knees; wives toasted their feet by the fires; while the men and youths were along at the pub, drinking hot-pokered cider, cutting cards for crib, and watching their wet boots steam.

But few cards were dealt or played that night. An apparition intervened. The door blew open to a gust of snow and a tall man strode into the bar. He seemed to the drinkers both unknown and familiar; he had a sharp tanned face, a nasal twang, and convinced of his welcome he addressed everyone by name, while they lowered their eyes and nodded. Slapping the bar, he ordered drinks all round, and then he began to talk.

Everyone, save the youths, remembered this man; now they studied the change within him. Years ago, as a pale and bony lad, he had been packed off to one of the Colonies, sent by subscription and the prayers of the Church, as many a poor boy before him. Usually they went, and were never heard from again, and their existence was soon forgotten. Now one of them had returned like a gilded ghost, successful and richly dressed, had come back to taunt the stay-at-homes with his boasting talk and money.

He had landed that morning, he said, at Bristol, from an Auckland mutton-boat. The carriage he'd hired had broken down in the snow, so he was finishing his journey on foot.

He was on his way to his parent's cottage to give them a Christmas surprise; another mile up the valley, another mile in the snow—he couldn't pass the old pub, now, could he?

He stood feet apart, his back to the bar, displaying himself to the company. Save for his yelping voice, the pub was silent, and the drinkers watched him closely. He'd done pretty well out there, he said, raised cattle, made a heap of money. It was easy enough if you just had the guts and weren't stuck in the bogs like some. . . . The old men listened, and the young men watched, with the oil lamps red in their eyes. . . .

He sent round more drinks and the men drank them down. He talked of the world and its width and richness. He lectured the old ones for the waste of their lives and the youths for their dumb contentment. They slogged for the Squire and the tenant-farmers for a miserable twelve bob a week. They lived on potatoes and by touching their caps, they hadn't a sovereign to rub between them, they saw not a thing save muck and each other—and perhaps Stroud on a Saturday night. Did they know what he'd done? what he'd seen? what he'd made? His brown face was aglow with whisky. He spread a sheaf of pound notes along the bar and fished a fat gold watch from his pocket. That's nothing, he said, that's only a part of it. They should see his big farm in New Zealand—horses, carriages, meat every day, and he never said 'sir' to no one.

The old men kept silent, but drank their free drinks and sniggered every so often. The youths in the shadows just gazed at the man, and gazed at his spinning watch, and as he grew more drunk they looked at each other, then stole away one by one. . . .

The weather outside had suddenly hardened into a blizzard of cutting snow; the night shut down to the blinding cold and the village curled up in its sheets. When the public house closed and turned down its lamps, the New Zealander was the last to leave. He refused a lantern, said he was born here, wasn't he? and paid for his bill with gold. Then he buttoned his coat, shouted goodnight, and strode up the howling valley. Warm with whisky and nearing home, he went singing up the hill. There were those in their beds who heard his last song, pitched wailing against the storm.

When he reached the stone-cross the young men were waiting, a bunched group, heads down in the wind.

'Well, Vincent?' they said; and he stopped, and stopped singing.

They hit him in turn, beat him down to his knees, beat him bloodily down in the snow. They beat and kicked him for the sake of themselves, as he lay there face down, groaning. Then they ripped off his coat, emptied his pockets, threw him over a wall, and left him. He was insensible now from his wounds and the drink; the storm blew all night across him. He didn't stir again from the place where he lay; and in the morning he was found frozen to death.

The police came, of course, but discovered nothing. Their enquiries were met by stares. But the tale spread quickly from mouth to mouth, was deliberately spread amongst us, was given to everyone, man and child, that we might learn each detail and hide it. The police left at last with the case unsolved; but neither we nor they forgot it. . . .

About ten years later an old lady lay dying, and towards the end she grew light-headed. The subject of her wandering leaked out somehow: she seemed to be haunted by a watch. 'The watch,' she kept mumbling, 'they maun find the watch. Tell the boy to get it hid.' A dark-suited stranger, with a notebook in his hand, appeared suddenly at her bedside. While she tossed and muttered, he sat and waited, head bent to her whispering mouth.

He was patient, anonymous, and never made any fuss; he just sat by her bed all day, his notebook open, his pencil poised, the blank pages like listening ears.

The old lady at last had a lucid moment and saw the stranger sitting beside her. 'Who's this?' she demanded of her hovering daughter. The girl leaned over the bed. 'It's all right, Mother,' said the daughter distinctly. 'It's only a police-station gentleman. He hasn't come to make any trouble. He just wants to hear about the watch.'

The old lady gave the stranger a sharp clear look and uttered not another word; she just leaned back on the pillow, closed her lips and eyes, folded her hands and died. It was the end of the weakness that had endangered her sons; and the dark-suited stranger knew it. He rose to his feet, put his notebook in his pocket, and tiptoed out of the room. This old and wandering dying mind had been their final chance. No other leads appeared after that, and the case was never solved.

But the young men who had gathered in that winter ambush continued to live among us. I saw them often about the village: simple jokers, hard-working, mild—the solid heads of families. They were not treated as outcasts, nor did they appear to live under any special stain. They belonged to the village and the village looked after them. They are all of them dead now anyway.

*　　*　　*

Grief or madness were not so private, though they were kept within the village, playing themselves out before our eyes to the accompaniment of lowered voices. There was the case of Miss Flynn, the Elcombe suicide, a solitary off-beat beauty, whose mute, distressed, life-abandoned image remains with me till this day.

Miss Flynn lived up on the other side of the valley in a cottage which faced the Severn, a cottage whose rows of tinted windows all burst into flame at sundown. She was tall, consumptive and pale as thistledown, a flock-haired pre-Raphaelite stunner, and she had a small wind-harp which played tunes to itself by swinging in the boughs of her apple trees. On walks with our Mother we often passed that way, and we always looked out for her. When she saw strangers coming she skipped at the sight of them—into her cellar or into their arms. Mother was evasive when we asked questions about her, and said, 'There are others more wicked, poor soul.'

Miss Flynn liked us boys, and gave us apples and stroked our hair with her long yellow fingers. We liked her too; in an eerie way—her skipping, her hair, her harp in the trees, her curious manners of speech. Her beauty for us was also remarkable, there was no one like her in the district; her long, stone-white and tapering face seemed as cool as a churchyard angel.

I remember the last time we passed her cottage, our eyes cocked as usual for her. She was sitting behind the stained-glass window, her face brooding in many colours. Our Mother called brightly; 'Yoo-hoo, Miss Flynn! Are you home? How you keeping, my dear?'

Miss Flynn came out with a skip to the door, stared down at her hands, then at us.

'Such cheeky boys,' I heard her say. 'The image of Morgan they are.' She lifted one knee and pointed her toe. 'I've been bad, Mrs Er,' she said.

She came swaying towards us, twisting her hair with her fingers and looking white as a daylight moon. Our Mother made a clucking, sympathetic sound, and said the west wind was bad for the nerves.

Miss Flynn embraced Tony with a kind of abstract passion and stared hard over our heads at the distance.

'I've been bad, Mrs Er—for the things I must do. It's my mother again, you know. I've been trying to keep her sick spirit from me. She don't let me alone at nights.'

Quite soon we were hurried off down the lane, although we were loth to go. 'The poor, poor soul,' Mother sighed to herself; 'and she half-gentry, too. . . .'

A few mornings later we were sitting round the kitchen, waiting for Fred Bates to deliver the milk. It must have been a Sunday because the breakfast was spoilt; and on weekdays that didn't matter. Everybody was grumbling; the porridge was burnt, and we hadn't yet had any tea. When Fred came at last he was an hour and a half late, and he had a milk-wet look in his eyes.

'Where were you, Fred Bates?' our sisters demanded; he'd never been late before. He was a thin, scrubby lad in his middle teens, with a head like a bottle-brush. But the cat didn't coil round his legs this morning, and he made no reply to the girls. He just ladled us out our usual jugful and kept sniffing and muttering 'God dammit.'

'What's up then, Fred?' asked Dorothy.

'Ain't nobody told you?' he asked. His voice was hollow, amazed, yet proud, and it made the girls sit up. They dragged him indoors and

130

poured him a cup of tea and forced him to sit down a minute. Then they all gathered round him with gaping eyes, and I could see they had sniffed an occurrence.

At first Fred could only blow hard on his tea and mutter, '*Who'd* a thought it?' But slowly, insidiously, the girls worked on him, and in the end they got his story. . . .

He'd been coming from milking; it was early, first light, and he was just passing Jones's pond. He'd stopped for a minute to chuck a stone at a rat—he got tuppence a tail when he caught one. Down by the lily-weeds he suddenly saw something floating. It was spread out white in the water. He'd thought at first it was a dead swan or something, or at least one of Jones's goats. But when he went down closer, he saw, staring up at him, the white drowned face of Miss Flynn. Her long hair was loose—which had made him think of a swan—and she wasn't wearing a stitch of clothes. Her eyes were wide open and she was staring up through the water like somebody gazing through a window. Well, he'd got such a shock he dropped one of his buckets, and the milk ran into the pond. He'd stood there a bit, thinking, 'That's Miss Flynn'; and there was no one but him around. Then he'd run back to the farm and told them about it, and they'd

131

come and fished her out with a hay-rake. He'd not waited to see any more, not he; he'd got his milk to deliver.

Fred sat for a while, sucking his tea, and we gazed at him with wonder. We all knew Fred Bates, we knew him well, and our girls often said he was soppy; yet only two hours ago, and only just down the lane, he'd seen drowned Miss Flynn with no clothes on. Now he seemed to exude a sort of salty sharpness so that we all wished to touch and taste him; and the excited girls tried to hold him back and make him go through his story again. But he finished his tea, sniffed hard, and left us, saying he'd still got his milk round to do.

The news soon spread around the village, and women began to gather at their gates.

'Have you heard?'

'No. What?'

'About poor Miss Flynn ... Been and drowned herself down in the pond.'

'You just can't mean it!'

'Yes. Fred Bates found her.'

'Yes—he just been drinking tea in our kitchen.'

'I can't believe it. I only saw her last week.'

'I know; I saw her just yesterday. I said, "Good moring, Miss Flynn"; and she said, "Good-morning, Mrs Ayres,"—you know,

132

'like she always did.'

'But she was down in the town, only Friday it was! I saw her in the Home-and-Colonial.'

'Poor, sad creature—whatever made her do it?'

'Such a lovely face she had.'

'So good to our boys. She was kindness itself. To think of her lying there.'

'She had a bit of a handicap, so they say.'

'You mean about those fellows?'

'No, more'n that.'

'What was it?'

'Ssssh!'

'Well, not everyone knows, of course. . . .'

Miss Flynn was drowned. The women looked at me listening. I stole off and ran down the lane. I was dry with excitement and tight with dread; I just wanted to see the pond. A group of villagers, including my sisters, stood gaping down at the water. The pond was flat and green and empty, and a smudge of milk clung to the reeds. I hid in the rushes, hoping not to be seen, and stared at that seething stain. This was the pond that had choked Miss Flynn. Yet strangely, and not by accident. She had come to it naked, alone in the night, and had slipped into it like a bed; she lay down there, and drew the water over her, and drowned quietly away in the

133

reeds. I gazed at the lily roots coiled deep down, at the spongy weeds around them. That's where she lay, a green foot under, still and all night by herself, looking up through the water as though through a window and waiting for Fred to come by. One of my knees began to quiver; it was easy to see her there, her hair floating out and her white eyes open, exactly as Fred Bates had found her. I saw her clearly, slightly magnified, and heard her vague dry voice: 'I've been bad, Mrs Er. It's my mother's spirit. She won't let me bide at night. . . .'

The pond was empty. She'd been carried home on a hurdle, and the women had seen to her body. But for me, as long as I can remember, Miss Flynn remained drowned in that pond.

As for Fred Bates, he enjoyed for a day a welcome wherever he went. He repeated his story over and over again and drank cups of tea by the dozen. But his fame turned bad, very suddenly; for a more sinister sequel followed. The very next day, on a visit to Stroud, he saw a man crushed to death by a wagon.

'Twice in two days,' the villagers said. 'He'll see the Devil next.'

Fred Bates was avoided after that. We crossed roads when we saw him coming. No

134

one would speak to him or look him in the
eyes, and he wasn't allowed to deliver milk
any more. He was sent off instead to work
alone in a quarry, and it took him years to re-
establish himself.

*   *   *

The murder and the drowning were long
ago, but to me they still loom large; the sharp
death-taste, tooth-edge of violence, the yield-
ing to the water of that despairing beauty, the
indignant blood in the snow. They occurred
at a time when the village was the world and
its happenings all I knew. The village in fact
was like a deep-running cave still linked to its
antic past, a cave whose shadows were clut-
tered by spirits and by laws still vaguely
ancestral. This cave that we inhabited looked
backwards through chambers that led to our
ghostly beginnings; and had not, as yet, been
tidied up, or scrubbed clean by electric light,
or suburbanized by a Victorian Church, or
papered by cinema screens.

It was something we just had time to inherit, to inherit and dimly know—the blood
and beliefs of generations who had been in
this valley since the Stone Age. That continuous contact has at last been broken, the

135

deeper caves sealed off for ever. But arriving, as I did, at the end of that age, I caught whiffs of something old as the glaciers. There were ghosts in the stones, in the trees, and the walls, and each field and hill had several. The elder people knew about these things and would refer to them in personal terms, and there were certain landmarks about the valley—tree-clumps, corners in woods—that bore separate, antique, half-muttered names that were certainly older than Christian. The women in their talk still used these names which are not used now any more. There was also a frank and unfearful attitude to death, and an acceptance of violence as a kind of ritual which no one accused or pardoned.

In our grey stone village, especially in winter, such stories never seemed strange. When I sat at home among my talking sisters, or with an old woman sucking her jaws, and heard the long details of hapless suicides, of fighting men loose in the snow, of witch-doomed widows disembowelled by bulls, of child-eating sows, and so on—I would look through the windows and see the wet walls streaming, the black trees bend in the wind, and I saw these things happening as natural convulsions of our landscape, and though dry-mouthed, I was never astonished.

Being so recently born, birth had no meaning; it was the other extreme that enthralled me. Death was absorbing, and I saw much of it; it was my childhood's continuous fare. Somebody else had gone, they had gone in the night, and nobody tried to hide it. Old women, bright-eyed, came carrying the news; the corpse was praised and buried; while Mother and the girls at their kitchen chorus went over the final hours. 'The poor old thing. She fought to the last. She didn't have the strength left in her.' They wept easily, sniffing, and healthily flushed; they could have been mourning the death of a dog.

Winter, of course, was the worst time for the old ones. Then they curled up like salted snails. We called one Sunday on the old Davies couple who lived along by the shop. It had been a cold wet January, a marrow-bone freezer, during which three old folk, on three successive Saturdays, had been carried off to their graves. Mr and Mrs Davies were ancient too, but they had a stubborn air of survival; and they used to watch each other, as I remember, with the calculating looks of card-players. This morning the women began to discuss the funerals, while we boys sat down by the fire. Mrs Davies was jaunty, naming each of the mourners and examining their bills of health. She rocked her white head, shot her husband a glance, and said she wondered who would be next.

The old man listened, fed some sticks to the fire, then knocked out his pipe on his leggings.

'You best fasten the windows, missus,' he said. 'The Old Bugger seems to snatch 'em week-ends.'

He wheezed at that, and coughed a bit, then relapsed into a happy silence. His wife considered him brightly for a moment, and then turned with a sigh to our mother.

'Once you had to run to keep up with him,' she said. 'You can talk to him now all right. He's no longer the way as I remember. The years have slowed him down.'

Her husband just cackled and stared at the fire-bars as though he'd still a few cards up his sleeve. . . .

A week or two later he took to his bed. He was bad and was said to be wasting. We went up again to the bank-side cottage to enquire how the old man was. Mrs Davies, looking frisky in a new yellow shawl, received us in her box-like kitchen—a tiny smoked cave in which had been gathered a lifetime of fragile trophies, including some oddments of china, an angel clock, a text on a string by the fire-place, a bust of Victoria, some broken tea-pots

138

and pipes, and an engraving of Redcoats at bay.

Mrs Davies was boiling a pot of gruel, her thin back bent like an eel-cage. She bade us sit down, stirred the pot madly, then sank into a wicker chair.

'He's bad,' she said, jerking her head upstairs, 'and you can't really wonder at it. He's had ammonia for years . . . his lungs is like sponges. He don't know it, but we reckon he's sinking.'

She handed us boys some hard peas to chew and settled to talk to our mother.

'It was like this, Mrs Lee. He took ill on the Friday. I sent for me daughter Madge. We fetched him two doctors, Dr Wills and Dr Packer, but they fell out over the operation. Dr Wills, you see, don't believe in cutting, so he gave him a course of treatment. But Dr Packer, he got into a pet over that, being a rigid one for the knife. But Albert wouldn't be messed about. He said he'd no mind to be butchered. "Give me a bit of boiled bacon and let me bide," he said. I'm with him there of course. It's true, you know—once you've been cut, you're never the same again.'

'Let me finish the gruel,' said Mother, standing up. 'You're trying to do too much.'

Mrs Davies surrendered the ladle vaguely,

139

and shook out her shawl around her.

'D'you know, Mrs Lee, I was setting here last night just counting all them as been took; and from Farmer Lusty's up to the Memorial I reckoned t'were nigh on a hunderd.' She folded her hands into a pious box and settled her eyes on the ceiling. 'Give me the strength to fight the world, and that what's to come upon us. . . .'

Later we were allowed to climb up the stairs and visit the old man in his bed. Mr Davies was sinking, that was only too clear. He lay in the ice-cold pokey bedroom, his breath coming rough and heavy, his thin brown fingers clutching the sheets like hooks of copper wire. His face was a skull wrapped in yellow paper, pierced by two brilliant holes. His hair had been brushed so that it stuck from his head like frosted grass on a stone.

'I've brought the boys to see you!' cried Mother; but Mr Davies made no answer; he just stared away at some shiny distance, at something we could not see. There was a long, long silence, smelling of cologne and bed-dust, of damp walls and apple-sweet fever. Then the old man sighed and shrank even smaller, a bright wetness against the pillow. He licked his lips, shot a glance at his wife, and gave a wheezy half-giggling cough.

140

'When I'm gone,' he said, 'see I'm decent, missus. Wrap up me doings in a red silk handkerchief....'

★   ★   ★

The wet winter days seemed at times unending, and quite often they led to self-slaughter. Girls jumped down wells, young men cut their veins, spinsters locked themselves up and starved. There was something spendthrift about such gestures, a scorn of life and complaining, and those who took to them were never censured, but were spoken about in a special voice as though their actions raised them above the living and defeated the misery of the world. Even so, such outbursts were often contagious and could lead to waves of throat-cutting; indeed, during one particularly gloomy season even the coroner did himself in.

But if you survived melancholia and rotting lungs it was possible to live long in this valley. Joseph and Hannah Brown, for instance, appeared to be indestructible. For as long as I could remember they had lived together in the same house by the common. They had lived there, it was said, for fifty years; which seemed to me for ever. They had raised a large family and sent them into the world, and had continued to live on alone, with nothing left of their noisy brood save some dog-eared letters and photographs.

The old couple were as absorbed in themselves as lovers, content and self-contained; they never left the village or each other's company, they lived as snug as two podded chestnuts. By day blue smoke curled up from their chimney, at night the red windows glowed; the cottage, when we passed it, said 'Here live the Browns', as though that were part of nature.

Though white and withered, they were active enough, but they ordered their lives without haste. The old woman cooked, and threw grain to the chickens, and hung out her washing on bushes; the old man fetched wood and chopped it with a billhook, did a bit of gardening now and then, or just sat on a seat outside his door and gazed at the valley, or slept. When summer came they bottled fruit, and when winter came they ate it. They did nothing more than was necessary to live, but did it fondly, with skill—then sat together in their clock-ticking kitchen enjoying their half-century of silence. Whoever called to see them was welcomed gravely, be it man or beast or child; and to me they resembled two

142

tawny insects, slow but deft in their movements; a little foraging, some frugal feeding,
then any amount of stillness. They spoke to
each other without raised voices, in short
chirrups as brief as bird-song, and when they
moved about in their tiny kitchen they did so
smoothly and blind, gliding on worn, familiar
rails, never bumping or obstructing each other.
They were fond, pink-faced, and alike as
cherries, having taken and merged, through
their years together, each other's looks and
accents.

It seemed that the old Browns belonged for
ever, and that the miracle of their survival
was made commonplace by the durability of
their love—if one should call it love, such a
balance. Then suddenly, within the space of
two days, feebleness took them both. It was as
though two machines, wound up and
synchronized, had run down at exactly the
same time. Their interdependence was so
legendary we didn't notice their plight at first.
But after a week, not having been seen about,
some neighbours thought it best to call. They
found old Hannah on the kitchen floor feeding her man with a spoon. He was lying in a
corner half-covered with matting, and they
were both too weak to stand. She had chopped
up a plate of peelings, she said, as she hadn't

143

been able to manage the fire. But they were all right really, just a touch of the damp; they'd do, and it didn't matter.

Well, the Authorities were told; the Visiting Spinsters got busy; and it was decided they would have to be moved. They were too frail to help each other now, and their children were too scattered, too busy. There was but one thing to be done; it was for the best; they would have to be moved to the Workhouse.

The old couple were shocked and terrified, and lay clutching each others hands. 'The Workhouse'—always a word of shame, grey shadow falling on the close of life, most feared by the old (even when called The Infirmary); abhorred more than debt, or prison, or beggary, or even the stain of madness.

Hannah and Joseph thanked the Visiting Spinsters but pleaded to be left at home, to be left as they wanted, to cause no trouble, just simply to stay together. The Workhouse could not give them the mercy they needed, but could only divide them in charity. Much better to hide, or die in a ditch, or to starve in one's familiar kitchen, watched by the objects one's life had gathered—the scrubbed empty table, the plates and saucepans, the cold grate, the white stopped clock. . . .

'You'll be well looked after,' the Spinsters said, 'and you'll see each other twice a week.' The bright busy voices cajoled with authority and the old couple were not trained to defy them. So that same afternoon, white and speechless, they were taken away to the Workhouse. Hannah Brown was put to bed in the Woman's Wing, and Joseph lay in the Men's. It was the first time, in all their fifty years, that they had ever been separated. They did not see each other again, for in a week they both were dead.

I was haunted by their end as by no other, and by the kind, killing Authority that arranged it. Divided, their life went out of them, so they ceased as by mutual agreement. Their cottage stood empty on the edge of the common, its front door locked and soundless. Its stones grew rapidly cold and repellent with its life so suddenly withdrawn. In a year it fell down, first the roof, then the walls, and lay scattered in a tangle of briars. Its decay was so violent and overwhelming, it was as though the old couple had wrecked it themselves.

Soon all that remained of Joe and Hannah Brown, and of their long close life together, were some grass-grown stumps, a garden gone wild, some rusty pots, and a dog-rose.

MOTHER

MY Mother was born near Gloucester, in the village of Quedgeley, sometime in the early 1880s. On her own mother's side she was descended from a long static line of Cotswold farmers who had been deprived of their lands through a monotony of disasters in which drink, simplicity, gambling and robbery played more or less equal parts. Through her father, John Light, the Berkeley coachman, she had some mysterious connection with the Castle, something vague and intimate, half-forgotten, who knows what? but implying a blood-link somewhere. Indeed, it was said that a retainer called Lightly led the murder of Edward II—at least, this was a local scholar's opinion. Mother accepted the theory with both shame and pleasure—as it has similarly confused me since.

But whatever the illicit grandeurs of her forebears, Mother was born to quite ordinary poverty, and was the only sister to a large family of boys, a responsibility she discharged somewhat wildly. The lack of sisters and daughters was something Mother always regretted; brothers and sons being her lifetime's lot.

She was a bright and dreamy child, it seemed, with a curious, hungry mind; and she was given to airs of incongruous elegance which never quite suited her background. She was the pride, none the less, of the village schoolmaster, who did his utmost to protect and develop her. At a time when country schooling was little more than a cane-whacking interlude in which boys picked up facts like bruises and the girls scarcely counted at all, Mr Jolly, the Quedgeley schoolmaster, found this solemn child and her ravenous questioning both rare and irre-sistible. He was an elderly man who had bat-tered the rudiments of learning into several generations of farmhands. But in Annie Light he saw a freak of intelligence which he felt bound to nurture and cherish.

'Mr Jolly was really educated,' Mother told us; 'and the pains he took with poor me.' She giggled. 'He used to stop after school to put me through my sums—I was never any good at figures. I can see him now, parading up and down, pulling at his little white whiskers. "Annie," he used to say, "you've got a lovely fist. You write the best essays in class. But you can't do sums. . . ." And I couldn't, either; they used to tie me in knots inside. But he was

147

patience itself; he *made* me learn; and he used to lend me all his beautiful books. He wanted me to train to be a teacher, you see. But of course Father wouldn't hear of it. . . .'

When she was about thirteen years old her mother was taken ill, so the girl had to leave school for good. She had her five young brothers and her father to look after, and there was no one else to help. So she put away her books and her modest ambitions as she was naturally expected to do. The schoolmaster was furious and called her father a scoundrel, but was helpless to interfere. 'Poor Mr Jolly,' said Mother, fondly. 'He never seemed to give up. He used to come round home when I was doing the washing and lecture me on Oliver Cromwell. He used to sit there so sad, saying it was a sinful shame, till Father used to dance and swear. . . .'

There was probably no one less capable of bringing up five husky brothers than this scatter-brained, half-grown girl. But she did what she could, at least. Meanwhile, she grew into tumble-haired adolescence, slap-dashing the housework in fits of abstraction and sliding into trances over the vegetables. She lived by longing rather than domestic law: Mr Jolly and his books had ruined her. During her small leisure hours she would put up her hair, squeeze her body into a tight-boned dress, and either sit by the window, or walk in the fields—getting poetry by heart, or sketching the landscape in a delicate snowflake scribble.

To the other village girls Mother was something of a case, yet they were curiously drawn towards her. Her strain of fantasy, her deranged sense of fun, her invention, satire and elegance of manner, must have intrigued and perplexed them equally. One gathered that there were also quarrels at times, jealousies, name-callings and tears. But there existed a coterie among the Quedgeley girls of which Mother was the exasperating centre. Books were passed round, excursions arranged, boys confounded by witty tongues. 'Beatie Thomas, Vi Phillips—the laughs we used to have. The things we did. We were *terrible.*'

When her brothers were big enough to look after themselves, Mother went into domestic service. Wearing her best straw hat and carrying a rope-tied box, seventeen and shapely, half-wistful, half-excited, she set out alone for that world of great houses which in those days absorbed most of her kind. As scullery-maid, housemaid, nursemaid, parlour-maid, in large manors all over the west, she saw luxuries and refinements she could never forget,

149

and to which in some ways she naturally belonged.

The idea of the Gentry, like love or the theatre, stayed to haunt her for the rest of her life. It haunted us too, through her. 'Real Gentry wouldn't hear of it,' she used to say; 'the Gentry always do it like this.' Her tone of voice, when referring to their ways, was reverent, genteel and longing. It proclaimed standards of culture we could never hope to attain and mourned their impossible perfections.

Sometimes, for instance, faced by a scratch meal in the kitchen, Mother would transform it in a trance of memory. A gleam would come to her hazy eyes and a special stance to her body. Lightly she would deploy a few plates on the table and curl her fingers airily. . . .

'For dining, they'd have every place just *so*; personal cruets for every guest. . . .' Grimly we settled to our greens and bacon: there was no way to stop her now. 'The silver and napery must be arranged in order, a set for each separate dish. . . .' Our old bent forks would be whisked into line, helter-skelter along the table. 'First of all, the butler would bring in the soup (scoop-scoop) and begin by serving the ladies. There'd be river-trout next, or fresh salmon (flick-flick) lightly sprinkled with herbs and sauces. Then some woodcock perhaps, or a guinea-fowl—oh, yes, and a joint as well. And a cold ham on the sideboard, too, if you wished. For the gentlemen only, of course. The ladies never did more than pick at their food—' 'Why not?' '—Oh, it wasn't thought proper. Then Cook would send in some violet cakes, and there'd be walnuts and fruit in brandy. You'd have wine, of course, with every dish, each served in a different glass. . . .' Stunned, we would listen, grinding our teeth and swallowing our empty hungers. Meanwhile Mother would have completely forgotten our soup, which then boiled over, and put out the fire.

But there were other stories of Big House life which we found somewhat less affronting. Glimpses of balls and their shimmering company, the chandeliers loaded with light. ('We cleared a barrel of candle-ends next morning.') And then Miss Emily's betrothal. ('What a picture she was—we were allowed a peep from the stairs. A man came from Paris just to do her hair. Her dress had a thousand pearls. There were fiddlers in black perched up in the gallery. The gentlemen all wore uniform. Then the dances—the Polka, the Two-Step, the Schottische—oh, dear, I was carried away. We were all of us up on the top landing, listening; I was wicked in those days, I know. I seized hold of the pantry-boy and said, "Come on Tom", and we danced up and down the passage. Then the Butler found us and boxed our ears. He was a terrible man, Mr Bee. . . .')

The long hard days the girls had of it then: rising before dawn, all feathered with sleep, to lay twenty or thirty fires; the sweeping, scrubbing, dusting and polishing that was done but to be done again; the scouring of pyramids of glass and silver; the scampering up and down stairs; and those irritable little bells that began ringing in tantrums just when you'd managed to put up your feet.

There was a £5-a-year wage, a 14-hour day, and a small attic for ravenous sleep: for the rest, the sub-grandees of the servants' hall with a caste-system more rigid than India's.

All the same, below-stairs was a lusty life, an underworld of warmth and plenty, huge meals served cosily cheek-by-jowl, with roast joints and porter for all. Ruled by a despotic or gin-mellow Butler and a severe or fun-fattened Cook, the young country girls and the grooms and the footmen stirred a seething broth together. There were pursuits down the passages, starched love in the laundry, smothered kisses behind green-baize doors—such flights and engagements filled the scrambling hours when the rows of brass bells were silent.

How did Mother fit in to all this, I wonder? And those neat-fingered parlour-queens, prim over-housemaids, reigning Cooks, raging Nannies, who ordered her labours—what could they have made of her? Mischievous, muddle-headed, full of brilliant fancies, half-witless, half touched with wonder; she was something entirely beyond their ken and must often have been their despair. But she was popular in those halls, a kind of mascot or clown; and she was beautiful, most beautiful at that time. She may not have known it, but her pictures reveal it; she herself seemed astonished to be noticed.

Two of her stories which reflect this astonishment I remember very well. Each is no more than an incident, but when she told them to us they took on a poignancy which prevented us from thinking them stale. I must have heard them many times, right on into her later years, but at each re-telling she flushed and shone, and looked down at her hands in amazement, recalling again those two magic encounters which raised her for a moment from Annie Light the housemaid to a throne of enamelled myrtles.

The first one took place at the end of the century, when Mother was at Gaviston

Court. 'It was an old house, you know; very rambling and dark; a bit primitive too in some ways. But they entertained a lot—not just Gentry, but all sorts, even black men too at times. The Master had travelled all round the world and he was a very distinguished gentleman. You never quite knew what you were going to run into—it bothered us girls at times.

'Well, one winter's night they had this big house-party and the place was packed right out. It was much too cold to use the outside privy, but there was one just along the passage. The staff wasn't supposed to use it, of course; but I thought, oh, I'll take a chance. Well, I'd just got me hand on the privy door when suddenly it flew wide open. And there, large as life, stood an Indian prince, with a turban, and jewels in his beard. I felt awful, you know—I was only a girl—I wished the ground to swallow me up. I just bobbed him a curtsy and said, "Pardon, your Highness"—I was paralysed, you see. But he only smiled, and then folded his hands, and bowed low, and said "Please madame to enter." So I held up my head, and went in, and sat down. Just like that. I felt like a Queen. . . .'

The second encounter Mother always described as though it had never happened—in

154

that special, morning, dream-telling voice that set it apart from all ordinary life. 'I was working at the time in a big red house at a place called Farnhamsurrey. On my Sundays off I used to go into Aldershot to visit my friend Amy Frost—Amy Hawkins that was, from Churchdown you know, before she got married, that is. Well, this particular Sunday I'd dressed up as usual, and I do think I looked a picture. I'd my smart lace-up boots, striped blouse and choker, a new bonnet and crochet-work gloves. I got into Aldershot far too early so I just walked about for a bit. We'd had rain in the night and the streets were shining, and I was standing quite alone on the pavement. When suddenly round the corner, without any warning, marched a full-dress regiment of soldiers. I stood transfixed; all those men and just me; I didn't know where to look. The officer in front—he had beautiful whiskers—raised his sword and cried out "Eyes right!" Then, would you believe, the drums started rolling, and the bagpipes started to play, and all those wonderful lads as they went swinging by snapped to attention and looked straight in my eyes. I stood all alone in my Sunday dress, it quite took my breath away. All those drums and pipes, and that salute just for me—I just cried, it was so exciting. . . .'

★   ★   ★

Later, our grandfather retired from his horses and went into the liquor business. He became host at The Plough, a small Sheepscombe inn, and when Grandmother died, a year or two afterwards, Mother left service to help him. Those were days of rough brews, penny ales, tuppenny rums, home-made cider, the staggers and violence. Mother didn't altogether approve of the life, but she entered the calling with spirit. 'That's where I learned the frog-march,' she'd say; 'and there were plenty of those who got it! Pug Sollars, for instance; the biggest bully in Sheepscombe—cider used to send him mad. He'd pick up the tables and lay about him like an animal while the chaps hid behind the piano. "Annie!" they'd holler, "for the Lord's sake save us!" I was the only one could handle Pug. Many's the time I've caught him by the collar and run him along the passage. Others, too— if they made me wild, I'd just throw them out in the road. Dad was too easy, so it was me had to do it. . . . They smirk when they see me now.'

The Plough Inn was built as one of the

smaller stages on the old coach road to Birdlip; but by Mother's time the road had
decayed and was no longer the main route to
anywhere. One or two carters, impelled by old
habits, still used the lane and the inn, and
Mother gave them ale and bacon suppers and
put them to sleep in the stables. Otherwise,
few travellers passed that way, and the lane
was mostly silent. So through the long afternoons Mother fell into dreams of idleness,
would dress in her best and sit out on the terrace, reading, or copying flowers. She was a
lonely young woman, mysteriously detached,
graceful in face and figure. Most of the village
boys were afraid of her, of her stormy temper,
her superior wit, her unpredictable mental
exercises.

Mother spent several odd years in that village pub, living her double life, switching
from bar-room rages to terrace meditations,
and waiting while her twenties passed.
Grandfather, on the other hand, spent his
time in the cellars playing the fiddle across his
boot. He held the landlordship of an inn to be
the same as Shaw's definition of marriage—as something combining the maximum of temptation with the maximum of
opportunity. So he seldom appeared except
late in the evening, when he'd pop up through

a hole in the floor, his clothes undone, his face streaming with tears, singing 'The Warrior's Little Boy'.

Mother stuck by him faithfully, handled the drunks, grew older and awaited deliverance. Then one day she read in a local paper: 'Widower (4 Children) Seeks Housekeeper.' She had had enough of Pug Sollars by now, and of fiddle-tunes in the cellar. She changed into her best, went out on to the terrace, sat down, and answered the advertisement. A reply came back, an appointment was made; and that's how she met my father.

*   *   *

When she moved into his tiny house in Stroud, and took charge of his four small children, Mother was thirty and still quite handsome. She had not, I suppose, met anyone like him before. This rather priggish young man, with his devout gentility, his airs and manners, his music and ambitions, his charm, bright talk and undeniable good looks, overwhelmed her as soon as she saw him. So she fell in love with him immediately, and remained in love for ever. And herself being comely, sensitive and adoring, she attracted my father also. And so he married her. And so later he left her—with his children and some more of her own.

When he'd gone, she brought us to the village and waited. She waited for thirty years. I don't think she ever knew what had made him desert her, though the reasons seemed clear enough. She was too honest, too natural for this frightened man; too remote from his tidy laws. She was, after all, a country girl; disordered, hysterical, loving. She was muddled and mischievous as a chimney-jackdaw, she made her nest of rags and jewels, was happy in the sunlight, squawked loudly at danger, pried and was insatiably curious, forgot when to eat or ate all day, and sang when sunsets were red. She lived by the easy laws of the hedgerow, loved the world and made no plans, had a quick holy eye for natural wonders and couldn't have kept a neat house for her life. What my father wished for was something quite different, something she could never give him—the protective order of an unimpeachable suburbia, which was what he got in the end.

The three or four years Mother spent with my father she fed on for the rest of her life. Her happiness at that time was something she guarded as though it must ensure his eventual return. She would talk about it almost in awe, not that it had ceased but that it had happened at all.

'He was proud of me then. I could make him laugh. "Nance, you're a killer," he'd say. He used to sit on the doorstep quite helpless with giggles at the stories and things I told him. He admired me too; he admired my looks; he really loved me, you know. "Come on, Nance," he'd say, "Take out your pins. Let your hair down—let's see it shine!" He loved my hair; it had gold lights in it then and it hung right down my back. So I'd sit in the window and shake it over my shoulders—it was so heavy you wouldn't believe—and he'd twist and arrange it so that it caught the sun, and then sit and just gaze and gaze. . . .

'Sometimes, when you children were all in bed, he'd clear all his books away—"Come on, Nance," he'd say, "I've had enough of them. Come and sing us a song!" We'd go to the piano, and I'd sit on his lap, and he'd play with his arms around me. And I'd sing him "Killarney" and "Only a Rose". They were both his favourites then. . . .'

When she told us these things it was yesterday and she held him again in her enchantment. His later scorns were stripped away and the adored was again adoring. She'd smile and look up the weed-choked path as though

160

she saw him coming back for more.

But it was over all right, he'd gone for good, we were alone and that was that. Mother struggled to keep us clothed and fed, and found it pretty hard going. There was never much money, perhaps just enough, the few pounds that Father sent us; but it was her own muddle-head that Mother was fighting, her panic and innocence, forgetfulness, waste, and the creeping tide of debt. Also her outbursts of wayward extravagance which splendidly ignored our needs. The rent, as I said, was only 3s. 6d. a week, but we were often six months behind. There would be no meat at all from Monday to Saturday, then on Sunday a fabulous goose; no coal or new clothes for the whole of the winter, then she'd take us all to the theatre; Jack, with no boots, would be expensively photographed, a new bedroom suite would arrive; then we'd all be insured for thousands of pounds and the policies would lapse in a month. Suddenly the iron-frost of destitution would clamp down on the house, to be thawed out by another orgy of borrowing, while harsh things were said by our more sensible neighbours and people ran when they saw us coming.

In spite of all this, Mother believed in

good fortune, and especially in newspaper competitions. She was also convinced that if you praised a firm's goods they would shower you with free samples and money. She was once paid five shillings for such a tribute which she had addressed to a skin-food firm. From then on she bombarded the market with letters, dashing off several each week. Ecstatically phrased and boasting miraculous cures, they elegantly hinted at new dawns opened up because of, or salvations due only to: headache-powderers, limejuice-bottlers, corset-makers, beef-extractors, sausage-stuffers, bust-improvers, eyelash-growers, soap-boilers, love-mongerers, statesmen, corn-plasterers, and Kings. She never got another penny from any of these efforts; but such was her style, her passion and conviction, that the letters were often printed. She had bundles of clippings lying all over the house, headed 'Grateful Sufferer' or 'After Years of Torture' or 'I Used to Groan Myself to Sleep till I Stumbled on Your Ointment'. . . . She used to read them aloud with a flush of pride, quite forgetting their original purpose.

Deserted, debt-ridden, flurried, bewildered, doomed by ambitions that never came off, yet our Mother possessed an indestructible gaiety which welled up like a thermal spring. Her laughing, like her weeping, was instantaneous and childlike, and switched without warning—or memory. Her emotions were entirely without reserve; she clouted you one moment and hugged you the next—to the ruin of one's ragged nerves. If she knocked over a pot, or cut her finger, she let out a blood-chilling scream—then forgot about it immediately in a hop and skip or a song. I can still seem to hear her blundering about the kitchen: shrieks and howls of alarm, an occasional oath, a gasp of wonder, a sharp command to things to stay still. A falling coal would set her hair on end, a loud knock make her leap and yell, her world was a maze of small traps and snares acknowledged always by cries of dismay. One couldn't help jumping in sympathy with her, though one learned to ignore these alarms. They were, after all, no more than formal salutes to the devils that dogged her heels.

Often, when working and not actually screaming, Mother kept up an interior monologue. Or she would absent-mindedly pick up your last remark and sing it back at you in doggerel. 'Give me some tart,' you might say, for instance. 'Give you some tart? Of course. . . . Give me some tart! O give me your heart! Give me your heart to keep! I'll guard it

163

well, my pretty Nell, As the shepherd doth guard his sheep, tra-la. . . .'

Whenever there was a pause in the smashing of crockery, and Mother was in the mood, she would make up snap verses about local characters that could stab like a three-pronged fork:

> *Mrs Okey*
> *Makes me chokey:*
> *Hit her with a mallet!—croquet.*

This was typical of their edge, economy and freedom. Mrs Okey was our local postmistress and an amiable, friendly woman; but my Mother would sacrifice anybody for a rhyme.

Mother, like Gran Trill, lived by no clocks, and unpunctuality was bred in her bones. She was particularly off-hand where buses were concerned and missed more than she ever caught. In the free-going days when only carrier-carts ran to Stroud she would often hold them up for an hour, but when the motor-bus started she saw no difference and carried on in the same old way. Not till she heard its horn winding down from Sheepscombe did she ever begin to get ready. Then she would cram on her hat and fly round the kitchen with habitual cries and howls.

'Where's my gloves? Where's my handbag? Damn and cuss—where's my shoes? You can't find a thing in this hole! Help me, you idiots—don't just jangle and jarl—you'll all make me miss it, I know. Scream! There it comes!—Laurie, run up and stop it. Tell 'em I won't be a minute. . . .'

So I'd tear up the bank, just in time as usual, while the packed bus steamed to a halt.

'. . . Just coming, she says. Got to find her shoes. Won't be a minute, she says. . . .'

Misery for me; I stood there blushing; the driver honked his horn, while all the passengers leaned out of the windows and shook their umbrellas crossly.

'Mother Lee again. Lost 'er shoes again. Come on, put a jerk in it there!'

Then sweet and gay from down the bank would come Mother's placating voice.

'I'm coming—yo-hoo! Just mislaid my gloves. Wait a second! I'm coming, my dears.'

Puffing and smiling, hat crooked, scarf dangling, clutching her baskets and bags, she'd come hobbling at last through the stinging-nettles and climb hiccuping into her seat. . . .

When neither bus nor carrier-cart were running, Mother walked the four miles to the shops, trudging back home with her baskets of groceries and scattering packets of tea in the mud. When she tired of this, she'd borrow Dorothy's bicycle, though she never quite mastered the machine. Happy enough when the thing was in motion, it was stopping and starting that puzzled her. She had to be launched on her way by running parties of villagers; and to stop she rode into a hedge. With the Stroud Co-op Stores, where she was a registered customer, she had come to a special arrangement. This depended for its success upon a quick ear and timing, and was a beautiful operation to watch. As she coasted downhill towards the shop's main entrance she would let out one of her screams; an assistant, specially briefed, would tear through the shop, out the side door, and catch her in his arms. He had to be both young and nimble, for if he missed her she piled up by the police-station.

*   *   *

Our Mother was a buffoon, extravagant and romantic, and was never wholly taken seriously. Yet within her she nourished a delicacy of taste, a sensibility, a brightness of spirit, which though continuously bludgeoned by the cruelties of her luck remained uncrushed and unembittered to the end. Wherever she got it from, God knows—or how she managed to preserve it. But she loved this world and saw it fresh with hopes that never clouded. She was an artist, a light-giver and an original, and she never for a moment knew it. . . .

My first image of my Mother was of a beautiful woman, strong, bounteous, but with a gravity of breeding that was always visible beneath her nervous chatter. She became, in a few years, both bent and worn, her healthy opulence quickly gnawed away by her later trials and hungers. It is in this second stage that I remember her best, for in this stage she remained the longest. I can see her prowling about the kitchen, dipping a rusk into a cup of tea, with hair loose-tangled and shedding pins, clothes shapelessly humped around her, eyes peering sharply at some revelation of the light, crying Ah or Oh or There, talking of Tonks or reciting Tennyson and demanding my understanding.

With her love of finery, her unmade beds, her litters of unfinished scrapbooks, her taboos, superstitions and prudishness, her remarkable dignity, her pity for the persecuted, her awe of the gentry, and her detailed knowledge of the family trees of all the Royal Houses of Europe, she was a disorganized mass of unreconciled denials, a servant girl born to silk. Yet in spite of all this, she fed our oafish wits with steady, imperceptible shocks of beauty. Though she tortured our patience and exhausted our nerves, she was, all the time, building up around us, by the unconscious revelations of her loves, an interpretation of man and the natural world so unpretentious and easy that we never recognized it then, yet so true that we never forgot it.

Nothing now that I ever see that has the edge of gold around it—the change of a season, a jewelled bird in a bush, the eyes of orchids, water in the evening, a thistle, a picture, a poem—but my pleasure pays some brief duty to her. She tried me at times to the top of my bent. But I absorbed from birth, as now I know, the whole earth through her jaunty spirit.

*　　　*　　　*

Not until I left home did I ever live in a house where the rooms were clear and carpeted, where corners were visible and window-

168

seats empty, and where it was possible to sit on a kitchen chair without first turning it up and shaking it. Our Mother was one of those obsessive collectors who spend all their time stuffing the crannies of their lives with a ballast of wayward objects. She collected anything that came to hand, she never threw anything away, every rag and button was carefully hoarded as though to lose it would imperil us all. Two decades of newspapers, yellow as shrouds, was the dead past she clung to, the years saved for my father, maybe something she wished to show him. . . . Other crackpot symbols also littered the house: chair-springs, boot-lasts, sheets of broken glass, corset-bones, picture-frames, fire-dogs, top-hats, chess-men, feathers, and statues without heads. Most of these came on the tides of unknowing, and remained as though left by a flood. But in one thing—old china— Mother was a deliberate collector, and in this had an expert's eye.

Old china to Mother was gambling, the bottle, illicit love, all stirred up together; the sensuality of touch and the ornament of a taste she was born to but could never afford. She hunted old china for miles around, though she hadn't the money to do so; haunted shops and sales with wistful passion, and by wheedling, guile and occasional freaks of chance carried several fine pieces home.

Once, I remember, there was a big auction at Bisley, and Mother couldn't sleep for the thought of its treasures.

'It's a splendid old place,' she kept telling us. 'The Delacourt family, you know. Very cultivated they were—or *she* was, at least. It would be a crime not to go and look.'

When the Sale-day arrived, Mother rose right early and dressed in her auction clothes.

We had a cold scratch breakfast—she was too nervy to cook—then she edged herself out through the door.

'I shall only be looking. I shan't buy, of course. I just wanted to see their Spode. . . .'

Guiltily she met our expressionless eyes, then trotted away through the rain. . . .

That evening, just as we were about to have tea, we heard her calling as she came down the bank.

'Boys! Marge—Doth! I'm home! Come and see!'

Mud-stained, flushed and just a little shifty, she came hobbling through the gate.

'Oh, you *should* have been there. Such china and glass. I never saw anything like it. Dealers, dealers all over the place—but I did 'em all in the eye. Look, isn't it beautiful? I just had to get it . . . and it only cost a few coppers.'

She pulled from her bag a bone cup and saucer, paper-thin, exquisite and priceless— except that the cup and its handle had parted company, and the saucer lay in two pieces.

'Of course, I could get those bits riveted,' said Mother, holding them up to the sky. The light on her face was as soft and delicate as the egg-shell chips in her hand.

At that moment two carters came staggering down the path with a huge packing-case on their shoulders.

'Put it there,' said Mother, and they dumped it in the yard, took their tip, and departed groaning.

'Oh dear,' she giggled, 'I'd quite forgotten. . . . *That* went with the cup and saucer. I had to take it, it was all one lot. But I'm sure we'll find it helpful.'

We broke open the crate with a blow from the chopper and gathered to inspect the contents. Inside was a ballcock, a bundle of stair-rods, an aigrette, the head of a spade, some broken clay-pipes, a box full of sheep's teeth, and a framed photograph of Leamington Baths. . . .

In this way and others, we got some beautiful china, some of it even perfect. I remember a Sèvres clock once, pink-crushed with angels, and a set of Crown Derby in gold, and some airy figures from Dresden or somewhere that were like pieces of bubble-blown sunlight. It was never quite clear how Mother came by them all, but she would stroke and dust them, smiling to herself, and place them in different lights; or just stop and gaze at them, broom in hand, and sigh and shake with pleasure. They were all to her as magic casements, some cracked, some gravelled with faults, but each opening out on that secret world she knew intuitively but could never visit. She couldn't keep any of them long, however. She just had time to look them up in books, to absorb their shapes and histories, then guilt and necessity sent her off to Cheltenham to sell them back to the dealers. Sometimes—but rarely—she made a shilling or two profit, which eased her mind a little. But usually her cry was 'Oh, dear, I *was* foolish! I should really have asked them double. . . .'

*   *   *

Mother's father had a touch with horses; she had the same with flowers. She could grow them anywhere, at any time, and they seemed to live longer for her. She grew them with rough, almost slap-dash love, but her hands possessed such an understanding of their needs they seemed to turn to her like another sun. She could snatch a dry root from field or hedgerow, dab it into the garden, give it a shake—and almost immediately it flowered. One felt she could grow roses from a stick or chair-leg, so remarkable was this gift.

Our terraced strip of garden was Mother's monument, and she worked it headstrong, without plan. She would never control or clear this ground, merely cherish whatever was there; and she was as impartial in her encouragement to all that grew as a spell of sweet sunny weather. She would force nothing, graft nothing, nor set things in rows; she welcomed self-seeders, let each have its head, and was the enemy of very few weeds. Consequently our garden was a sprouting jungle and never an inch was wasted. Syringa shot up, laburnum hung down, white roses smothered the apple tree, red flowering-currants (smelling sharply of foxes) spread entirely along one path; such a chaos of blossom as amazed the bees and bewildered the birds in the air. Potatoes and cabbages were planted at random among foxgloves, pansies and pinks. Often some species would entirely capture the garden—forget-me-nots one year, hollyhocks the next, then a sheet of harvest poppies. Whatever it was, one let it grow. While Mother went creeping around the wilderness, pausing to tap some odd bloom on the head, as indulgent, gracious, amiable and inquisitive as a queen at an orphanage.

Our kitchen extended this outdoor profusion, for it was always crammed with bunches. In the green confines of that shadowy place, stockaded by leaves and flowers, the sun filtering dimly through the plant-screened windows, I often felt like an ant in a jungle overwhelmed by its opulent clusters. Almost anything that caught her wandering eye, Mother gathered and brought indoors. In bottles, tea-pots, dishes and jugs, in anything old or beautiful, she'd put roses, beech-boughs, parsley, hellebore, garlic, cornstalks and rhubarb. She also grew plants in whatever would hold them—saucepans, tea-caddies or ash tins. Indeed, she once raised a fine crop of geraniums in a cast-iron water-softener. We boys had found it thrown away in a wood—but only she knew what use to give it.

*   *   *

Although there was only one man in my mother's life—if he could ever be said to have been in it—she often grew sentimental about her girlhood suitors and liked to tell of their vanquished attentions. The postman she rejected because of his wig, the butcher who bled from her scorn, the cowman she'd shoved into Sheepscombe brook to cool his troublesome fires—there seemed many a man up and down the valleys whose love she once had blasted. Sometimes, out walking, or trudging from Stroud with our heads to the blowing rain, some fat whiskered farmer or jobbing builder would go jingling past in his trap. Then Mother would turn and watch him go, and shake the rain from her hat. 'You know, I could have married that man,' she'd murmur; 'if only I'd played my cards right. . . .'

Mother's romantic memories may not have all been reliable, for their character frequently changed. But of the stories she told us, about herself and others, the one of the Blacksmith and Toffee-Maker was true. . . .

Once, she said, in the village of C—, there lived a lovelorn blacksmith. For years he had loved a local spinster, but he was shy, as most blacksmiths are. The spinster, who eked out a

175

poor existence by boiling and selling toffee, was also lonely, in fact desperate for a husband, but too modest and proud to seek one. With the years the spinster's desperation grew, as did the blacksmith's speechless passion.

Then one day the spinster stole into the church and threw herself down on her knees. 'O Lord!' she prayed, 'please be mindful of me, and send me a man to marry!'

Now the blacksmith by chance was up in the belfry, mending the old church clock. Every breathless word of the spinster's entreaties rose clearly to where he was. When he heard her praying, 'Please send me a man!' he nearly fell off the roof with excitement. But he kept his head, tuned his voice to Jehovah's, and boomed 'Will a blacksmith do?'

'Ern a man's better than nern, dear Lord!' cried the spinster gratefully.

At which the blacksmith ran home, changed into his best, and caught the spinster on her way out of church. He proposed, and they married, and lived forever contented, and used his forge for boiling their toffee.

*   *   *

In trying to recapture the presence of my

Mother I am pulling at broken strings. The years run back through the pattern of her confusions. Her flowers and songs, her un-shaken fidelities, her attempts at order, her relapses into squalor, her near madness, her crying for light, her almost daily weeping for her dead child-daughter, her frisks and gaie-ties, her fits of screams, her love of man, her hysterical rages, her justice towards each of us children—all these rode my mother and sat on her shoulders like a roosting of ravens and doves. Equally I remember her occasional blooming, when she became secretly beautiful and alone. And those summer nights—we boys in bed—when the green of the yew trees filled the quiet kitchen, and she would change into her silk, put on her bits of jewellery, and sit down to play the piano.

She did not play well; her rough fingers stumbled, they trembled to find the notes—yet she carried the music with little rushes of grace, half-faltering surges of feeling, that went rippling out through the kitchen win-dows like signals from a shuttered cage. Soli-tary, eyes closed, in her silks and secrets, tearing arpeggios from the yellow keys, yield-ing, through dusty but golden chords, to the peak of that private moment, it was clearly then, in the twilit tenderness she created, that

177

the man should have returned to her.

I would lie awake in my still-light bedroom and hear the chime of the piano below, a ragged chord, a poignant pause, then a twinkling wagtail run. Brash yet melancholy, coarse yet wistful, it would rise in a jangling burst, then break and shiver as soft as water and lap round my listening head. She would play some waltzes, and of course 'Killarney'; and sometimes I would hear her singing—a cool lone voice, uncertainly rising, addressed to her own reflection. They were sounds of peace, half-edged with sleep, yet disturbing, almost shamefully moving. I wanted to run to her then, and embrace her as she played. But somehow I never did.

*   *   *

As time went on, Mother grew less protesting. She had earned acquiescence and wore it gratefully. But as we children grew up, leaving home in turn, so her idiosyncracies spread; her plant-pots and newspapers, muddles and scrapbooks extended further throughout the house. She read more now and never went to bed, merely slept upright in a chair. Her nights and days were no longer divided nor harassed by the wants of children.

She would sleep for an hour, rise and scrub the floor, or go wooding in the middle of the night. Like Granny Trill, she began to ignore all time and to do what she would when she wished. Even so, whenever we returned for a visit, she was ready, fires burning, to greet us. . . .

I remember coming home in the middle of the war, arriving about two in the morning. And there she was, sitting up in her chair, reading a book with a magnifying glass. 'Ah, son,' she said—she didn't know I was coming—'come here, take a look at this. . . .' We examined the book, then I went up to bed and fell into an exhausted sleep. I was roused at some dark cold hour near dawn by Mother climbing the stairs. 'I got you your dinner, son,' she said, and planked a great tray on the bed. Aching with sleep, I screwed my eyes open—veg soup, a big stew and a pudding. The boy had come home and he had to have supper, and she had spent half the night preparing it. She sat on my bed and made me eat it all up—she didn't know it was nearly morning.

So with the family gone, Mother lived as she wished, knowing she'd done what she could: happy to see us, content to be alone, sleeping, gardening, cutting out pictures, writing us letters about the birds, going for bus-rides, visiting friends, reading Ruskin or the lives of the saints. Slowly, snugly, she grew into her background, warm on her grassy bank, poking and peering among the flowery bushes, dishevelled and bright as they. Serenely unkempt were those final years, free from conflict, doubt or dismay, while she reverted gently to a rustic simplicity as a moss-rose reverts to a wild one.

Then suddenly our absent father died—cranking his car in a Morden suburb. And with that, his death, which was also the death of hope, our Mother gave up her life. Their long separation had come to an end, and it was the coldness of that which killed her. She had raised his two families, faithfully and alone: had waited thirty-five years for his praise. And through all that time she had clung to one fantasy—that aged and broken, at last in need, he might one day return to her. His death killed that promise, and also ended her reason. The mellow tranquillity she had latterly grown forsook her then forever. She became frail, simple-minded and returned to her youth, to that girlhood which had never known him. She never mentioned him again, but spoke to shades, saw visions, and then she died.

We buried her in the village, under the edge of the beechwood, not far from her four-year-old daughter.

WINTER AND SUMMER

THE seasons of my childhood seemed (of course) so violent, so intense and true to their nature, that they have become for me ever since a reference of perfection whenever such names are mentioned. They possessed us so completely they seemed to change our nationality; and when I look back to the valley it cannot be one place I see, but village-winter or village-summer, both separate. It becomes increasingly easy in urban life to ignore their extreme humours, but in those days winter and summer dominated our every action, broke into our houses, conscripted our thoughts, ruled our games, and ordered our lives.

Winter was no more typical of our valley than summer, it was not even summer's opposite; it was merely that other place. And somehow one never remembered the journey towards it; one arrived, and winter was here. The day came suddenly when all details were different and the village had to be rediscovered. One's nose went dead so that it hurt to breathe, and there were jigsaws of frost on the window. The light filled the house with a green polar glow; while outside—in the invisible world—there was a strange hard silence, or a metallic creaking, a faint throbbing of twigs and wires.

The kitchen that morning would be full of steam, billowing from kettles and pots. The outside pump was frozen again, making a sound like broken crockery, so that the girls tore icicles from the eaves for water and we drank boiled ice in our tea.

'It's wicked,' said Mother, 'The poor, poor birds.' And she flapped her arms with vigour.

She and the girls were wrapped in all they had, coats and scarves and mittens; some had the shivers and some drops on their noses, while poor little Phyllis sat rocking in a chair holding her chilblains like a handful of bees.

There was an iron-shod clatter down the garden path and the milkman pushed open the door. The milk in his pail was frozen solid. He had to break off lumps with a hammer.

'It's murder out,' the milkman said. 'Crows worryin' the sheep. Swans froze in the lake. An' tits droppin' dead in mid-air. . . .' He drank his tea while his eyebrows melted, slapped Dorothy's bottom, and left.

'The poor, poor birds,' Mother said again.

They were hopping around the windowsill,

183

calling for bread and fats—robins, black-birds, wood-peckers, jays, never seen together save now. We fed them for awhile, amazed at their tameness, then put on our long wool mufflers.

'Can we go out, Mother?'

'Well, don't catch cold. And remember to get some wood.'

First we found some old cocoa-tins, punched them with holes, then packed them with smouldering rags. If held in the hand and blown on occasionally they would keep hot for several hours. They were warmer than gloves, and smelt better too. In any case, we never wore gloves. So armed with these, and full of hot breakfast, we stepped out into the winter world.

It was a world of glass, sparkling and motionless. Vapours had frozen all over the trees and transformed them into confections of sugar. Everything was rigid, locked-up and sealed, and when we breathed the air it smelt like needles and stabbed our nostrils and made us sneeze.

Having sucked a few icicles, and kicked the water-butt—to hear its solid sound—and breathed through the frost on the window-pane, we ran up into the road. We hung around, waiting for something to happen. A dog trotted past like a ghost in a cloud, panting his aura around him. The distant fields in the low weak sun were crumpled like oyster shells.

Presently some more boys came to join us, wrapped like Russians, with multi-coloured noses. We stood round in a group and just gasped at each other, waiting to get an idea. The thin ones were blue, with hunched up shoulders, hands deep in their pockets, shivering. The fat ones were rosy and blowing like whales; all of us had wet eyes. What should we do? We didn't know. So the fat ones punched the thin ones, who doubled up, saying, 'Sod you.' Then the thin ones punched the fat ones, who half-died coughing. Then we all jumped up and down for a bit, flapped our arms, and blew on our cocoatins.

'What we goin' to *do*, then, eh?'

We quietened down to think. A shuddering thin boy, with his lips drawn back, was eating the wind with his teeth. 'Giddy up,' he said suddenly, and sprang into the air and began whipping himself, and whinnying. At that we all galloped away down the road, bucking and snorting, tugging invisible reins, and lashing away at our hindquarters.

Now the winter's day was set in motion and

we rode through its crystal kingdom. We examined the village for its freaks of frost, for anything we might use. We saw the frozen spring by the side of the road, huge like a swollen flower. Water-wagtails hovered above it, nonplussed at its silent hardness, and again and again they dropped down to drink, only to go sprawling in a tumble of feathers. We saw the stream in the valley, black and halted, a tarred path threading through the willows. We saw trees lopped-off by their burdens of ice, cow-tracks like pot-holes in rock, quiet lumps of sheep lickering the spiky grass with their black and rotting tongues. The church clock had stopped and the weather-cock was frozen, so that both time and the winds were stilled; and nothing, we thought, could be more exciting than this; interference by a hand unknown, the winter's No to routine and laws—sinister, awesome, welcome.

'Let's go an' 'elp Farmer Wells,' said a fat boy.

'You can—I ain't,' said a thin one.

'If you don't, I'll give thee a clip in the yer'ole.'

'Gurt great bully.'

'I ain't.'

'You be.'

So we went to the farm on the lip of the village, a farm built from a long-gone abbey. Wells, the farmer, had a young sick son more beautiful than a girl. He waved from his window as we trooped into the farmyard, and wouldn't live to last out the winter. The farmyard muck was brown and hard, dusted with frost like a baked bread-pudding. From the sheds came the rattle of morning milking, chains and buckets, a cow's deep sigh, stumbling hooves and a steady munching.

'Wan' any 'elp, Mr Wells?' we asked.

He crossed the yard with two buckets on a yoke; as usual he was dressed in dung. He was small and bald, but had long sweeping arms that seemed stretched from his heavy labours.

'Well, come on,' he said. 'But no playing the goat. . . .'

Inside the cowsheds it was warm and voluptuous, smelling sweetly of milky breath, of heaving hides, green dung and udders, of steam and fermentations. We carried cut hay from the heart of the rick, packed tight as tobacco flake, with grass and wild flowers juicily fossilized within—a whole summer embalmed in our arms.

I took a bucket of milk to feed a calf. It opened its mouth like a hot wet orchid. It began to suck at my fingers, gurgling in its throat and raising its long-lashed eyes. The milk had been skimmed for making butter and the calf drank a bucket a day. We drank the same stuff at home sometimes; Mr Wells sold it for a penny a jug.

When we'd finished the feeding we got a handful of apples and a baked potato each. The apples were so cold they stung the teeth, but the potatoes were hot, with butter. We made a dinner of this then scuffled back to the village, where we ran into the bully Walt Kerry.

'Wan' a know summat?' he asked.

'What?'

'Shan't tell ya.'

He whistled a bit, and cleaned his ears. He gave out knowledge in very small parcels.

'Well, if you *wan*'a know, I may's well. . . .'

We waited in a shivering lump.

'Jones's pond is bearing,' he said at last. 'I bin a-slidin' on it all mornin'. Millions bin comin' wi 'orses an' traps an' skates an' things an' all.'

We tore away down the frosty lane, blood up and elbows well out.

'Remember I told ya. An' I got there fust. An' I'll be back when I've 'ad me tea!'

We left him standing in the low pink sun, small as a cankered rose, spiky, thorny, a thing of dread, only to be encountered with shears.

We could hear the pond as we ran down the hill, the shouts that only water produces, the squeal of skates, the ring of the ice and its hollow heaving grumble. Then we saw it; black and flat as a tray, the skaters rolling round it like marbles. We broke into a shout and charged upon it and fell sprawling in all directions. This magic substance, with its deceptive gifts, was something I could never master. It put wings on my heels and gave me the motions of Mercury, then threw me down on my nose. Yet it chose its own darlings, never the ones you supposed, the dromedary louts of the schoolroom, who came skating past with one leg in the air, who twirled and simpered, and darted like swifts; and never fell once—not they.

I was one of the pedestrians, and we worked up a slide across the polished darkness. So smooth that to step on it was to glide away, while the valley slid past like oil. You could also lie prone and try to swim on the ice, kicking your arms and legs. And you saw deep down, while in that position, little bubbles like cold green stars, jagged ominous cracks, dead ribbons of lilies, drowned bulrushes loaded like rockets.

The frozen pond on such a winter's evening was a very treadmill of pleasure. Time was uncounted; sensations almost sexual; we played ourselves into exhaustion. We ran and slid till we dripped with sweat; our scarves were pearled with our breath. The reeds and horse-tails at the pond's edge smelt as pungent as old men's fingers. Hanging branches of willow, manacled in the ice, bloomed like lilac in the setting sun. Then the frost moon rose through the charcoal trees and we knew that we'd played too long.

We had promised Mother we would fetch some wood. We had to get some each day in winter. Jack and I, hands in pockets, mooched silently up the lane; it was night now, and we were frightened. The beech wood was a cavern of moonlight and shadows, and we kept very close together.

The dead sticks on the ground were easily seen, glittering with the night's new frost. As we ripped them from the earth, scabbed with soil and leaves, our hands began to burn with the cold. The wood was silent and freezing hard, white and smelling of wolves. Such a night as lost hunters must have stared upon when first they wandered north into the Ice Age. We thought of caves, warm skins and fires, grabbed our sticks and tore off home.

Then there were 'Where've - you - beens? Never - minds, Oh - Dears, and Come - by - the - fire - you - look - half - dead. First the long slow torment as our hands thawed out, a quiet agony of returning blood. Worse than toothache it was; I sat there sobbing, but gradually the pain wave passed. Then we had jugs of tea, hot toast and dripping; and later our sisters came.

'It was murder in Stroud. I fell down twice—in the High Street—and tore my stockings. I'm sure I showed everything. It was terrible, Ma. And a horse went through Maypole's window. And old Mr Fowler couldn't get down the hill and had to sit on his bottom and slide. It's freezing harder than ever now. We won't none of us be able to budge tomorrow.'

They sat at their tea and went on talking about it in their sing-song disaster voices. And we boys were content to know the winter had come, total winter, the new occupation. . . .

Later, towards Christmas, there was heavy snow, which raised the roads to the top of the hedges. There were millions of tons of the lovely stuff, plastic, pure, all-purpose, which nobody owned, which one could carve or tunnel, eat, or just throw about. It covered the hills and cut off the villages, but nobody

191

thought of rescues; for there was hay in the barns and flour in the kitchens, the women baked bread, the cattle were fed and sheltered—we'd been cut off before, after all.

The week before Christmas, when snow seemed to lie thickest, was the moment for carol-singing; and when I think back to those nights it is to the crunch of snow and to the lights of the lanterns on it. Carol-singing in my village was a special tithe for the boys, the girls had little to do with it. Like hay-making, black-berrying, stone-clearing and wishing-people-a-happy-Easter, it was one of our seasonal perks.

By instinct we knew just when to begin it; a day too soon and we should have been unwelcome, a day too late and we should have received lean looks from people whose bounty was already exhausted. When the true moment came, exactly balanced, we recognized it and were ready.

So as soon as the wood had been stacked in the oven to dry for the morning fire, we put on our scarves and went out through the streets, calling loudly between our hands, till the various boys who knew the signal ran out from their houses to join us.

One by one they came stumbling over the snow, swinging their lanterns around their heads, shouting and coughing horribly.

'Coming carol-barking then?'

We were the Church Choir, so no answer was necessary. For a year we had praised the Lord out of key, and as a reward for this service—on top of the Outing—we now had the right to visit all the big houses, to sing our carols and collect our tribute.

To work them all in meant a five-mile foot journey over wild and generally snowed-up country. So the first thing we did was to plan our route; a formality, as the route never changed. All the same, we blew on our fingers and argued; and then we chose our Leader. This was not binding, for we all fancied ourselves as Leaders, and he who started the night in that position usually trailed home with a bloody nose.

. Eight of us set out that night. There was Sixpence the Tanner, who had never sung in his life (he just worked his mouth in Church); the brothers Horace and Boney, who were always fighting everybody and always getting the worst of it; Clergy Green, the preaching maniac; Walt the bully, and my two brothers. As we went down the lane other boys, from other villages, were already about the hills, bawling 'Kingwenslush', and shouting through keyholes 'Knock on the knocker!

Ring at the Bell! Give us a penny for singing so well!' They weren't an approved charity as we were, the Choir; but competition was in the air.

Our first call as usual was the house of the Squire, and we trouped nervously down his drive. For light we had candles in marmalade-jars suspended on loops of string, and they threw pale gleams on the towering snowdrifts that stood on each side of the drive. A blizzard was blowing, but we were well wrapped up, with Army puttees on our legs, woollen hats on our heads, and several scarves around our ears.

As we approached the Big House across its white silent lawns, we too grew respectfully silent. The lake near by was stiff and black, the waterfall frozen and still. We arranged ourselves shuffling around the big front door, then knocked and announced the Choir.

A maid bore the tidings of our arrival away into the echoing distances of the house, and while we waited we cleared our throats noisily. Then she came back, and the door was left ajar for us, and we were bidden to begin. We brought no music, the carols were in our heads. 'Let's give 'em "Wild Shepherds",' said Jack. We began in confusion, plunging into a wreckage of keys, of different words and tempo; but we gathered our strength; he who sang loudest took the rest of us with him, and the carol took shape if not sweetness.

This huge stone house, with its ivied walls, was always a mystery to us. What were those gables, those rooms and attics, those narrow windows veiled by the cedar trees? As we sang 'Wild Shepherds' we craned our necks, gaping into that lamplit hall which we had never entered; staring at the muskets and untenanted chairs, the great tapestries furred by dust—until suddenly, on the stairs, we saw the old Squire himself standing and listening with his head on one side.

He didn't move until we'd finished; then slowly he tottered towards us, dropped two coins in our box with a trembling hand, scratched his name in the book we carried, gave us each a long look with his moist blind eyes, then turned away in silence.

As though released from a spell, we took a few sedate steps, then broke into a run for the gate. We didn't stop till we were out of the grounds. Impatient, at last, to discover the extent of his bounty, we squatted by the cow-sheds, held our lanterns over the book, and saw that he had written 'Two Shillings'. This was quite a good start. No one of any worth in the district would dare to give us less than the

Squire.

So with money in the box, we pushed on up the valley, pouring scorn on each other's performance. Confident now, we began to consider our quality and whether one carol was not better suited to us than another. Horace, Walt said, shouldn't sing at all; his voice was beginning to break. Horace disputed this and there was a brief token battle—they fought as they walked, kicking up divots of snow, then they forgot it, and Horace still sang.

Steadily we worked through the length of the valley, going from house to house, visiting the lesser and the greater gentry—the farmers, the doctors, the merchants, the majors and other exalted persons. It was freezing hard and blowing too; yet not for a moment did we feel the cold. The snow blew into our faces, into our eyes and mouths, soaked through our puttees, got into our boots, and dripped from our woollen caps. But we did not care. The collecting-box grew heavier, and the list of names in the book longer and more extravagant, each trying to outdo the other.

Mile after mile we went, fighting against the wind, falling into snowdrifts, and navigating by the lights of the houses. And yet we never saw our audience. We called at house after house; we sang in courtyards and porches, outside windows, or in the damp gloom of hallways; we heard voices from hidden rooms; we smelt rich clothes and strange hot food; we saw maids bearing in dishes or carrying away coffee-cups; we received nuts, cakes, figs, preserved ginger, dates, cough-drops and money; but we never once saw our patrons. We sang as it were at the castle walls, and apart from the Squire, who had shown himself to prove that he was still alive, we never expected it otherwise.

As the night drew on there was trouble with Boney. 'Noël', for instance, had a rousing harmony which Boney persisted in singing, and singing flat. The others forbade him to sing it at all, and Boney said he would fight us. Picking himself up, he agreed we were right, then he disappeared altogether. He just turned away and walked into the snow and wouldn't answer when we called him back. Much later, as we reached a far point up the valley, somebody said 'Hark!' and we stopped to listen. Far away across the fields from the distant village came the sound of a frail voice singing, singing 'Noël', and singing it flat—it was Boney, branching out on his own.

We approached our last house high up on the hill, the place of Joseph the farmer. For him we had chosen a special carol, which was about the other Joseph, so that we always felt that singing it added a spicy cheek to the night. The last stretch of country to reach his farm was perhaps the most difficult of all. In these rough bare lanes, open to all winds, sheep were buried and wagons lost. Huddled together, we tramped in one another's footsteps, powdered snow blew into our screwed-up eyes, the candles burnt low, some blew out altogether, and we talked loudly above the gale.

Crossing, at last, the frozen mill-stream—whose wheel in summer still turned a barren mechanism—we climbed up to Joseph's farm. Sheltered by trees, warm on its bed of snow, it seemed always to be like this. As always it was late; as always this was our final call. The snow had a fine crust upon it, and the old trees sparkled like tinsel.

We grouped ourselves round the farmhouse porch. The sky cleared, and broad streams of stars ran down over the valley and away to Wales. On Slad's white slopes, seen through the black sticks of its woods, some red lamps still burned in the windows.

Everything was quiet; everywhere there was the faint crackling silence of the winter night. We started singing, and we were all moved by the words and the sudden trueness of our voices. Pure, very clear, and breathless we sang:

As Joseph was a walking
He heard an angel sing;
'This night shall be the birth-time
Of Christ the Heavenly King.

He neither shall be bornèd
In Housen nor in hall,
Nor in a place of paradise
But in an ox's stall. . . .'

And 2,000 Christmasses became real to us then; the houses, the halls, the places of paradise had all been visited; the stars were bright to guide the Kings through the snow; and across the farmyard we could hear the beasts in their stalls. We were given roast apples and hot mince-pies, in our nostrils were spices like myrrh, and in our wooden box, as we headed back for the village, there were golden gifts for all.

*   *   *

Summer, June summer, with the green back on earth and the whole world unlocked and seething—like winter, it came suddenly and one knew it in bed, almost before waking up; with cuckoos and pigeons hollowing the woods since daylight and the chipping of tits in the pear-blossom.

On the bedroom ceiling, seen first through sleep, was a pool of expanding sunlight—the lake's reflection thrown up through the trees by the rapidly climbing sun. Still drowsy, I watched on the ceiling above me its glittering image reversed, saw every motion of its somnambulant waves and projections of the life upon it. Arrows ran across it from time to time, followed by the far call of a moorhen; I saw ripples of light around each root of the bulrushes, every detail of the lake seemed there. Then suddenly the whole picture would break into pieces, would be smashed like a molten mirror and run amok in tiny globules of gold, frantic and shivering; and I would hear the great slapping of wings on water, building up a steady crescendo, while across the ceiling passed the shadows of swans taking off into the heavy morning. I would hear their cries pass over the house and watch the chaos of light above me, till it slowly settled and re-collected its stars and resumed the lake's still image.

Watching swans take off from my bedroom

ceiling was a regular summer wakening. So I woke and looked out through the open window to a morning of cows and cockerels. The beech trees framing the lake and valley seemed to call for a Royal Hunt; but they served equally well for climbing into, and even in June you could still eat their leaves, a tight-folded salad of juices.

Outdoors, one scarcely knew what had happened or remembered any other time. There had never been rain, or frost, or cloud; it had always been like this. The heat from the ground climbed up one's legs and smote one under the chin. The garden, dizzy with scent and bees, burned all over with hot white flowers, each one so blinding an incandescence that it hurt the eyes to look at them.

The villagers took summer like a kind of punishment. The women never got used to it. Buckets of water were being sluiced down paths, the dust was being laid with grumbles, blankets and mattresses hung like tongues from the windows, panting dogs crouched under the rain-tubs. A man went by and asked 'Hot enough for 'ee?' and was answered by a worn-out shriek.

In the builder's stable, well out of the sun, we helped to groom Brown's horse. We smelt the burning of his coat, the horn of his hooves, his hot leather harness and dung. We fed him on bran, dry as a desert wind, till both we and the horse half-choked. Mr Brown and his family were going for a drive, so we wheeled the trap into the road, backed the blinkered horse between the shafts, and buckled his jingling straps. The road lay deserted in its layer of dust and not a thing seemed to move in the valley. Mr Brown and his best-dressed wife and daughter, followed by his bowler-hatted son-in-law, climbed one by one into the high sprung trap and sat there with ritual stiffness.

'Where we goin' then, Father?'

'Up the hill, for some air.'

'Up the hill? He'll drop down dead.'

'Bide quiet,' said Mr Brown, already dripping with sweat, 'Another word, and you'll go back 'ome.'

He jerked the reins and gave a flick of the whip and the horse broke into a saunter. The women clutched their hats at the unexpected movement, and we watched them till they were out of sight.

When they were gone there was nothing else to look at, the village slipped back into silence. The untarred road wound away up the valley, innocent as yet of motor-cars, wound empty away to other villages, which lay empty too, the hot day long, waiting for the sight of a stranger.

We sat by the roadside and scooped the dust with our hands and made little piles in the gutters. Then we slid through the grass and lay on our backs and just stared at the empty sky. There was nothing to do. Nothing moved or happened, nothing happened at all except summer. Small heated winds blew over our faces, dandelion seeds floated by, burnt sap and roast nettles tingled our nostrils together with the dull rust smell of dry ground. The grass was June high and had come up with a rush, a massed entanglement of species, crested with flowers and spears of wild wheat, and coiled with clambering vetches, the whole of it humming with blundering bees and flickering with scarlet butterflies. Chewing grass on our backs, the grass scaffolding the sky, the summer was all we heard; cuckoos crossed distances on chains of cries, flies buzzed and choked in the ears, and the saw-toothed chatter of mowing-machines drifted on waves of air from the fields.

We moved. We went to the shop and bought sherbet and sucked it through sticks of liquorice. Sucked gently, the sherbet merely dusted the tongue; too hard, and you choked with sweet powders; or if you blew back through the tube the sherbet-bag burst and you disappeared in a blizzard of sugar. Sucking and blowing, coughing and weeping, we scuffled our way down the lane. We drank at the spring to clean our mouths, then threw water at each other and made rainbows. Mr Jones's pond was bubbling with life, and covered with great white lilies—they poured from their leaves like candle-fat, ran molten, then cooled on the water. Moorhens plopped, and dab-chicks scooted, insects rowed and skated. New-hatched frogs hopped about like flies, lizards gulped in the grass. The lane itself was crusted with cow-dung, hard baked and smelling good.

We met Sixpence Robinson among the bulrushes, and he said, 'Come and have some fun.' He lived along the lane just past the sheepwash in a farm cottage near a bog. There were five in his family, two girls and three boys, and their names all began with S. There was Sis and Sloppy, Stosher and Sammy, and our good friend Sixpence the Tanner. Sis and Sloppy were both beautiful girls and used to hide from us boys in the gooseberries. It was the brothers we played with: and Sammy, though a cripple, was one of the most agile lads in the village.

Their's was a good place to be at any time,

and they were good to be with. (Like us, they had no father; unlike ours, he was dead.) So today, in the spicy heat of their bog, we sat round on logs and whistled, peeled sticks, played mouth-organs, dammed up the stream and cut harbours in the cool clay banks. Then we took all the pigeons out of their dovecots and ducked them in the water-butt, held them under till their beaks started bubbling then threw them up in the air. Splashing spray from their wings they flew round the house, then came back to roost like fools. (Sixpence had a one-eyed pigeon called Spike who he boasted could stay under longest, but one day the poor bird, having broken all records, crashed for ever among the cabbages.)

When all this was over, we retired to the paddock and played cricket under the trees. Sammy, in his leg-irons, charged up and down. Hens and guinea-fowl took to the trees. Sammy hopped and bowled like murder at us, and we defended our stumps with our lives. The cracked bat clouting; the cries in the reeds; the smells of fowls and water; the long afternoon with the steep hills around us watched by Sloppy still hid in the gooseberries—it seemed down here that no disasters could happen, that nothing could ever touch us. This was Sammy's and Sixpence's; the

place past the sheepwash, the hide-out
unspoiled by authority, where drowned
pigeons flew and cripples ran free; where it
was summer, in some ways, always.

★ ★ ★

Summer was also the time of these: of
sudden plenty, of slow hours and actions, of
diamond haze and dust on the eyes, of the valley in post-vernal slumber; of burying birds
out of seething corruption; of Mother sleeping heavily at noon; of jazzing wasps and dra-
gonflies, haystooks and thistle-seeds, snows of
white butterflies, skylarks' eggs, bee-orchids
and frantic ants; of wolf-cub parades, and
boy-scout's bugles; of sweat running down
the legs; of boiling potatoes on bramble fires,
of flames glass-blue in the sun; of lying naked
in the hill-cold stream; begging pennies for
bottles of pop; of girls' bare arms and unripe
cherries, green apples and liquid walnuts; of
fights and falls and new-scabbed knees, sobbing pursuits and flights; of picnics high up in
the crumbling quarries, of butter running like
oil, of sunstroke, fever, and cucumber peel
stuck cool to one's burning brow. All this, and
the feeling that it would never end, that such
days had come for ever, with the pump drying

up and the water-butt crawling, and the chalk ground hard as the moon. All sights twice-brilliant and smells twice-sharp, all game-days twice as long. Double charged as we were, like the meadow ants, with the frenzy of the sun, we used up the light to its last violet drop, and even then couldn't go to bed.

When darkness fell, and the huge moon rose, we stirred to a second life. Then boys went calling along the roads, wild slit-eyed animal calls, Walt Kerry's naked nasal yodel, Boney's jackal scream. As soon as we heard them we crept outdoors, out of our stifling bedrooms, stepped out into moonlight warm as the sun to join our chalk-white, moon-masked gang.

Games in the moon. Games of pursuit and capture. Games that the night demanded. Best of all, Fox and Hounds—go where you like, and the whole of the valley to hunt through. Two chosen boys loped away through the trees and were immediately swallowed in shadow. We gave them five minutes, then set off after them. They had churchyard, farmyard, barns, quarries, hilltops and woods to run to. They had all night, and the whole of the moon, and five miles of country to hide in. . . .

Padding softly, we ran under the melting

207

stars, through sharp garlic woods, through blue blazed fields, following the scent by the game's one rule, the question and answer cry. Every so often, panting for breath, we paused to check on our quarry. Bullet heads lifted, teeth shone in the moon. 'Whistle-or-'OLLER! Or - we - shall - not - FOLLER!' It was a cry on two notes, prolonged. From the other side of the hill, above white fields of mist, the faint fox-cry came back. We were off again then, through the waking night, among sleepless owls and badgers, while our quarry slipped off into another parish and would not be found for hours.

Round about midnight we ran them to earth, exhausted under a haystack. Until then we had chased them through all the world, through jungles, swamps and tundras, across pampas plains and steppes of wheat and plateaux of shooting stars, while hares made love in the silver grasses, and the large hot moon climbed over us, raising tides in my head of night and summer that move there even yet.

SICK BOY

As a child I used to boast the rare distinction of having been christened twice. The second time, which took place in church, was a somewhat rowdy affair; I was three years old and I cheeked the parson and made free with the holy water. But my first anointing was much more solemn and occurred immediately after my birth. I had entered the world in doubt and silence, a frail little lifeless lump; and the midwife, after one look at my worn-out face, said I wouldn't last the day. Everybody agreed, including the doctor, and they just waited for me to die.

My Mother however, while resigned to my loss, was determined I should enter heaven. She remembered those tiny anonymous graves tucked away under the churchyard laurels, where quick-dying infants—behind the vicar's back—were stowed secretly among the jam-jars. She said the bones of her son should rest in God's own ground and not rot with those pitiful heathens. So she summoned the curate, who came and called out my Adam, baptized me from a tea-cup, admitted me to the Church, and gave me three names to die with.

This flurried christening proved unnecessary, however. Something—who knows what?—some ancestral toughness maybe, saw me safely through the first day. I remained seriously ill for many months, inert, unnoticing, one of life's bad debts, more or less abandoned by all. 'You never moved or cried,' said my Mother, 'You just lay where I put you, like a little image, staring up at the ceiling all day.' In that motionless swoon I was but a clod, a scarce-breathing parcel of flesh. For a year I lay prone to successive invasions, enough to mop up an orphanage— I had diphtheria, whooping-cough, pleurisy, double pneumonia, and congestion of the bleeding lungs. My Mother watched, but could not help me; waited, but could not hope. In those days young children dropped dead like chickens, their diseases not well understood; families were large as though by compensation; at least a quarter were not expected to survive. My father had buried three of his children already, and was quite prepared to do the same by me.

But secretly, silently, aided by unknown forces, I hung on—though it was touch and go. My most perilous moment came when I was eighteen months old, at the hands of Mrs

Moore, a neighbour. My mother was in bed for the birth of my brother—we were all born at home those days. Mrs Moore, a negress, had been called in to help, to scrub the children and to cook them soups. She was a jolly, eye-bulging, voodoo-like creature who took charge of us with primitive casualness. While still in her care I entered a second bout of pneumonia. What followed I was told much later. . . .

It seems that brother Tony was but two days born and Mother just beginning to take notice. Eleven-year-old Dorothy came upstairs to see her, played awhile with the baby, nibbled some biscuits, then sat in the window and whistled.

'How you all getting on?' asked Mother.

'Oh, all right,' said Dorothy.

'You behaving yourselves?'

'Yes, Ma.'

'And what you all up to?'

'Nothing much.'

'Where's Marjorie then?'

'Out in the yard.'

'And Phyllis?'

'She's peeling spuds.'

'What about the others?'

'Harold's cleaning his trolly. And Jack and Frances is sitting on the steps.'

211

'And Laurie? . . . How's Laurie?'

'Oh, Laurie's dead.'

'What!'

'He turned yellow. They're laying him out . . .'

Giving one of her screams, Mother leapt out of bed.

'No one's going to lay out our Laurie!'

Gasping, she groped her way downstairs and staggered towards the kitchen: and lo, there I was, stretched naked on the table, yellow, just as Dorothy said. Mrs Moore, humming gaily, was sponging my body as though preparing a chicken for dinner.

'What you think you're doing?' my Mother shouted.

'Poor boy, he's gone,' crooned the negress. 'Gone fled to the angels—thought I'd wash him for the box—just didn't want to bother you, mum.'

'You cruel wicked woman! Our Laurie ain't dead—just look at his healthy colour.'

Mother plucked me from the table, wrapped me up in a blanket, and carried me back to my cot—cursing Mrs Moore for a snatcher of bodies and asking the Saints what they thought they were up to. Somehow, I lived—though it was a very near thing, a very near thing indeed. So easy to have succumbed

212

to Mrs Moore's cold sponge. Only Dorothy's boredom saved me.

★   ★   ★

It was soon after this that my sister Frances died. She was a beautiful, fragile, dark-curled child, and my Mother's only daughter. Though only four, she used to watch me like a nurse, sitting all day beside my cot and talking softly in a special language. Nobody noticed that she was dying herself, they were too much concerned with me. She died suddenly, silently, without complaint, in a chair in the corner of the room. An ignorant death which need never have happened—and I believe that she gave me her life.

But at least she was mourned. Not a day passed afterwards but that Mother shed some tears for her. Mother also grew jealous for the rest of us, more careful that we should survive. So I grew to be, not a pale wasting boy, but sickly in another way, switching regularly from a swaggering plumpness—a tough equality with other boys—to a monotonous return of grey-ghosted illness, hot and cold, ugly-featured and savage. When I was well I could hold my own; no one spared me, because I didn't look delicate. But when I was ill, I just disappeared from the scene and remained out of sight for weeks. If it was summer when the fever caught me, I lay and sweated in my usual bed, never quite sure which of us was ill, me or the steaming weather. But in winter a fire was lit in the bedroom, and then I knew I was ill indeed. Washbasins could freeze, icicles hang from the ornaments, our bedrooms remained normally unheated; but the lighting of a fire, especially in Mother's room, meant that serious illness had come.

As soon as I recognized the returning face of my sickness—my hands light as feathers, a swaying in the head and lungs full of pulsing thorns—the first thing I did was to recall my delusions and send messages to the anxious world. As I woke to the fever I thought of my subjects, and their concern always gave me comfort. Signals in morse, tapped out on the bed-rail, conveyed brief and austere intelligences. 'He is ill.' (I imagined the first alarm.) 'He has told his Mother.' (Some relief.) 'He is fighting hard.' (Massed prayers in the churches.) 'He is worse.' (Cries of doom in the streets.) There were times when I was almost moved to tears as the thought of my anxious people, the invisible multitudes up and down the land joined in grief at this threat to their King. How piteously they awaited each sombre bulletin, and how brave I was meanwhile. Certainly I took pains to give them something to be anxious about, but I also bid them be strong. 'He wishes no special arrangements made. Only bands and tanks. A parade or two. And perhaps a three minutes' silence.'

This would occupy my first morning, with the fever still fresh; but by nightfall I was usually raving. My limbs went first, splintering like logs, so that I seemed to grow dozens of arms. Then the bed no longer had limits to it and became a desert of hot wet sand. I began to talk to a second head laid on the pillow, my own head once removed; it never talked back, but just lay there grinning very coldly into my eyes. The walls of the bedroom were the next to go; they began to bulge and ripple and roar, to flap like pastry, melt like sugar, and run bleeding with hideous hues. Then out of the walls, and down from the ceiling, advanced a row of intangible smiles; easy, relaxed, in no way threatening at first, but going on far too long. Even a maniac's smile will finally waver, but these just continued in silence, growing brighter, colder, and ever more humourless till the sick blood roared in my veins. They were Cheshire-cat smiles, with no face or outlines, and I could see the room clearly through them. But they hung above me like a stain on the air, a register of smiles in space, smiles without pity, smiles without love, smiling smiles of unsmiling smileness; not even smiles of strangers but smiles of no one, expanding in brilliant silence, persistent, knowing, going on and on . . . till I was screaming and beating the bed-rails.

At my scream all the walls shook down like a thunderclap and everything was normal again. The kitchen door opened, feet thumped up the stairs and the girls bustled into the room. 'He's been seeing them faces again,' they whispered. 'It's all right!' they bawled, 'There, there! You won't see any more. Have a nice jug of lemon.' And they mopped me, and picked up the bedclothes. I lay back quietly while they fussed around; but what could I say to them? That I hadn't seen faces—that I'd only seen smiles? I tried that, but it got me nowhere.

Later, as the red night closed upon me, I was only barely conscious. I heard myself singing, groaning, talking, and the sounds were like hands on my body. Blood boiled, flesh crept, teeth chattered and clenched, my knees came up to my mouth; I lay in an evil swamp of sweat which alternately steamed and froze me. My shirt was a kind of enveloping sky wetly wrapping my goosy skin, and across which, at intervals, hot winds from Africa and Arctic blizzards blew. All objects in the room became molten again, and the pictures repainted themselves; things ran about, changed shape, grew monstrous, or trailed off into limitless distances. The flame of the candle threw shadows like cloaks which made everything vanish in turn, or it drew itself up like an ivory saint, or giggled and collapsed in a ball. I heard voices that couldn't control themselves, that either whispered just out of sound, or suddenly boomed some great echoing word, like 'Shovel!' or 'Old-men's-ears!' Such a shout would rouse me with terrible echoes, as though a piano had just been kicked by a horse.

It was myself, no doubt, who spoke these words, and the monologue went on for hours. Sometimes I deliberately answered back, but mostly I lay and listened, watching while the room's dark crevices began to smoke their ash-white nightmares. . . . Such a night of fever slowed everything down as though hot rugs had been stuffed in a clock. I went gliding away under the surface of sleep, like a porpoise in tropic seas, heard the dry house echoing through caves of water, followed caverns through acres of dreams, then emerged after fathoms and years of experience, of complex lives and deaths, to find that the moon on the window had not moved an inch, that the world was not a minute older.

Between this sleeping and waking I lived ten generations and grew weak on my long careers, but when I surfaced at last from its endless delirium the real world seemed suddenly dear. While I slept it had been washed of fever and sweetened, and now wrapped me like a bell of glass. For a while, refreshed, I heard its faintest sounds: streams running, trees stirring, birds folding their wings, a hill-sheep's cough, a far gate swinging, the breath of a horse in a field. Below me the kitchen made cosy murmurs, footsteps went up the road, a voice said Goodnight, a door creaked and closed—or a boy suddenly hollered, animal clear in the dark, and was answered far off by another. I lay moved to stupidity by these precious sounds as though I'd just got back from the dead. Then the fever returned as it always did, the room began its whisper and dance, the burnt-down candle spat once and shuddered, and I saw its wick fold and go out. . . . Then darkness hit me, a corroding darkness, a darkness packed like a box, and a row of black lanterns swung down from the ceiling and floated towards me, smiling. And once more I was hammering the bed-rails in terror, screaming loudly for sisters and light.

*   *   *

Such bouts of delirium were familiar visitations, and my family had long grown used to them. Jack would enquire if I needed to groan quite so much, while Tony examined me with sly speculation; but for the most part I was treated like a dog with distemper and left to mend in my own good time. The fevers were dramatic, sudden and soaring, but they burnt themselves out very quickly. There would follow a period of easy convalescence, during which I lived on milk custards and rusks; then I'd begin to feel bored, I'd get up and go out, start a fight, and my sickness was closed. Apart from the deliriums, which puzzled and confused me, I never felt really ill; and in spite of the whispers of scarred lungs and T.B., it never occurred to me I might die.

Then one night, while sweating through another attack, which seemed no different from any of the others, I was given a shock which affected me with an almost voluptuous awe. As usual my fever had flared up sharply, and I was tossing in its accustomed fires, when I woke up, clear-headed, somewhere in the middle of the night, to find the whole family round my bed. Seven pairs of eyes stared in dread surmise, not at me but at something in me. Mother stood helplessly wringing her hands, and the girls were silently weeping. Even Harold, who could usually shrug off emotion, looked pale and strained in the candlelight.

I was surprised by their silence and the look in their eyes, a mixture of fear and mourning. What had suddenly brought them in the dark of the night to stand blubbing like this around me? I felt warm and comfortable, completely relaxed, and amused as though somehow I'd fooled them. Then they all started whispering, around me, about me, across me, but never directly to me.

'He's never been like this before,' said one. 'Hark at his awful rattle.'

'He never had that ghastly colour, either.'

'It's cruel—the poor little mite.'

'Such a gay little chap he was, boo-hoo.'

'There, there, Phyl; don't you fret.'

'D'you think the vicar would come at this hour?'

'Someone better run and fetch him.'

'We'd better knock up Jack Halliday, too. He could bike down and fetch the doctor.'

'We'll have to sit up, Ma. His breathing's horrible.'

'Perhaps we should wire his dad . . .'

Perfectly conscious, I heard all this, and was tempted to join in myself. But their strangeness of tone compelled my silence, some peculiar threat in their manner, and a kind of fearful reverence in their eyes and voices as though they saw in me shades of the tomb. It was then that I knew I was very ill; not by pain, for my body felt normal. Silently the girls began to prepare for their vigil, wrapping their shawls around them. 'You go get some rest, Ma—we'll call you later.' They disposed themselves solemnly round the bed, folded their hands in their laps, and sat watching my face with their hollow eyes for the first signs of fatal change. Held by the silence of those waiting figures, in that icy mid-hour of the night, it came to me then, for the first time in my life, that it was possible I might die.

I remember no more of that sombre occasion, I think I just fell asleep—my eyelids closing on a shroud of sisters which might well have been my last sight on earth. When I woke next morning to their surprise, the crisis

221

was apparently over. And save for that midnight visitation, and for the subsequent behaviour of the village, I would never have known my danger.

I remained in Mother's bedroom for many weeks, and a wood-fire burned all day. Schoolfriends, as though on a pilgrimage, came in their best clothes to bring me flowers. Girls sent me hen's-eggs pencilled with kisses; boys brought me their broken toys. Even my schoolteacher (whose heart was of stone) brought me a bagful of sweets and nuts. Finally Jack, unable to keep the secret any longer, told me I'd been prayed for in church, just before the collections, twice, on successive Sundays. My cup was full, I felt immortal; very few had survived that honour.

This time my convalescence was even more indulgent. I lived on Bovril and dry spongecakes. I was daily embalmed with camphorated oils and hot-poulticed with Thermogene. Lying swathed in these pungent and peppery vapours, I played through my hours and days, my bed piled high with beads and comics, pressed flowers, old cartridges, jackknives, sparking-plugs, locusts, and several stuffed linnets.

I took every advantage of my spoiled condition and acted simple when things got tough. Particularly when it came to taking my medicine, a hell-draught of unspeakable vileness.

It was my sister's job to get this down, and they would woo me with outstretched spoon.

'Now come on, laddie—One! Two! Three! . . .'

'You can clean out the jam-pot after. . . .'

'We'll peg up your nose. You won't taste it at all.'

I crossed my eyes and looked vacant.

'Be a good boy. Just this once. Come on.'

'Archie says No,' I said.

'What?'

'Archie,' I said, 'does not want the dose. Archie does not like the dose. And Archie will not have the dose. Says Archie.'

'Who's Archie?' they whispered, shaking their heads at each other. They usually left me then.

*   *   *

After fever my body and head felt light, like a piece of dew-damp vegetable. The illness had emptied me so completely now I seemed bereft of substance. Being so long in that sunless, fever-spent room, I was filled with extraordinary translations. I felt white and blood-drained, empty of organs, transparent to colour and sound, while there passed through my flesh the lights of the window, the dust-changing air, the fire's bright hooks, and the smooth lapping tongues of the candle. Heat, reflections, whispers, shadows, played around me as though I was glass. I seemed to be bodiless, printed flat on the sheets, insubstantial as a net in water. What gross human wastes, dull jellies, slack salts I had been purged of I could not say; but my senses were now tuned to such an excruciating awareness that they vibrated to every move of the world, to every shift and subsidence both outdoors and in, as though I were renewing my entire geography.

When I woke in the mornings, damp with weakness, the daylight was milk of paradise; it came through the windows in beaming tides, in currents of green and blue, bearing debris of bird-song, petals, voices and the running oils of the sky. Its light washed the room of night and nightmare and showed me the normal day, so that waking was a moment of gratitude that savages must have felt. The bedroom objects removed their witch-masks and appeared almost sheepishly ordinary. The boarded walls shone with grains and knots; the mirror recorded facts; the pictures, framed in the morning's gold, restored me their familiar faces. I sighed and stretched like a washed-up sailor who feels the earth safe beneath him, wild seas wiped away, green leaves around, deliverance miraculously gained.

So each morning at dawn I lay in a trance of thanks. I sniffed the room and smelt its feathers, the water in the wash-jug, the dust in the corners, kind odours of glass and paper, the dry stones facing the windowsills, bees bruising the geranium leaves, the pine in the pencil beside my bed, the dead candle and the fire in the matchstick. But I also sensed, without needing to look, the state of the early day: the direction of the wind, how the trees were blowing, that there were cows in the fields or not, whether the garden gate was open or shut, whether the hens had yet been fed, the weight of the clouds in the invisible sky and the exact temperature of the air. As I lay in my bed I could sense the whole valley by the surfaces of my skin, the turn of the hour, the set of the year, the weather and the life to come. A kind of pantheist grandeur made me one with the village, so that I felt part of its destination; and washed of my fevers, ice-cold but alive, it seemed I would never lose it again. . . .

225

Then Mother would come carolling up-stairs with my breakfast, bright as a wind-blown lark.

'I've boiled you an egg, and made you a nice cup of cocoa. And cut you some lovely thin bread and butter.'

The fresh boiled egg tasted of sun-warmed manna, the cocoa frothed and steamed, and the bread and butter—cut invalid fashion—was so thin you could see the plate through it. I gobbled it down, looking weak and sorry, while Mother straightened the bed, gave me my pencil and drawing-book, my beads and toys, and chattered of treats to come.

'I'm going to walk into Stroud and buy you a paint-box. And maybe some liquorice all-sorts. All kinds of people have been asking about you. Even Miss Cohen!—just fancy that.'

Mother sat on the bed and looked at me proudly. All was love; and I could do no wrong. When I got up I would not have to chop any firewood, and nobody would be cross for a month. Oh, the fatal weakness that engaged me then, to be always and forever ill. . . .

*   *   *

Pneumonia was the thing for which I was best known, and I made a big drama out of it. But it was not by any means my only weapon, I collected minor diseases also, including, in the space of a few short years, bouts of shingles, chicken-pox, mumps, measles, ring-worm, adenoids, nose-bleed, nits, ear-ache, stomach-ache, wobbles, bends, scarlet-fever and catarrhal deafness.

Then finally, as though to round the lot off, I suffered concussion of the brain. I was knocked down by a bicycle one pitch-dark night and lay for two days unconscious. By the time I came to, all battered and scabbed, one of my sisters was in love with the bicy-clist—a handsome young stranger from Sheepscombe way who had also knocked down my Mother.

But my boyhood career of shocks and fevers confirmed one thing at least: had I been delicate I would surely have died, but there was no doubt about my toughness. Those were the days, as I have already said, when children faded quickly, when there was little to be done, should the lungs be affected, but to burn coal-tar and pray. In those cold valley cottages, with their dripping walls, damp beds and oozing floors, a child could sicken and die in a year, and it was usually the strongest who went. I was not strong; I was simply tough, self-inoculated by all the plagues. But sometimes, when I stop to think about it, I feel it must have been a very close call.

Strangely enough it was not illness, but the accident, which I believe most profoundly marked me. That blow in the night, which gave me concussion, scarred me, I think, for ever—put a stain of darkness upon my brow and opened a sinister door in my brain, a door through which I am regularly visited by messengers whose words just escape me, by glimpses of worlds I can never quite grasp, by grief, exultation and panic. . . .

THE UNCLES

Our family was large, even by the full-bred standards of those days, and we were especially well-endowed with uncles. Not so much by their numbers as by their qualities of behaviour, which transformed them for us boys into figures of legend, and filled the girls with distress and excitement. Uncle George—our father's brother—was a thin, whiskered rogue, who sold newspapers in the streets, lived for the most part in rags, and was said to have a fortune in gold. But on my Mother's side there were these five more uncles: squat, hard-hitting, heavy-drinking heroes whom we loved and who were the kings of our youth. For the affection we bore them and the pride we took in them, I hope they'll not be displeased by what follows.

Grandfather Light—who had the handsomest legs of any coachman in Gloucestershire—raised his five sons in a world of horses; and they inherited much of his skill. Two of them fought against the Boers; and all five were cavalrymen in the First World War, where they survived the massacres of Mons and Ypres, quick-witted their way through some others, and returned at last to peace and salvation with shrapnel in each of their bodies. I remember them first as khaki ghosts coming home on leave from the fighting, square and huge with their legs in puttees, smelling sweetly of leather and oats. They appeared as warriors stained with battle; they slept like the dead all day; then blackened their boots and Brassoed their buttons and returned again to the war. They were men of great strength, of bloody deeds, a fist of uncles aimed at the foe, riders of hell and apocalypse, each one half-man, half-horse.

Not until after the war did that brotherhood of avengers detach itself in my mind, so that I was able to see each one separate and human and to know at last who they were. The sons of John Light, the five Light brothers, illuminated many a local myth, were admired for their wildness, their force of arms, and for their leisurely, boasting wit. 'We come from the oldest family in the world. We're down in the Book of Genesis. The Almighty said, "Let there be Light"—and *that* was long afore Adam. . . .'

The uncles were all of them bred as coachmen and intended to follow their father; but the Army released them to a different world, and by the time I was old enough to register what they were up to only one worked with horses, the others followed separate careers; one with trees, one with motors, another with ships, and the last building Canadian railways.

★   ★   ★

Uncle Charlie, the eldest, was most like my grandfather. He had the same long face and shapely gaitered legs, the same tobacco-kippered smell about him, the same slow story-telling voice heavy with Gloucester bass-notes. He told us long tales of war and endurance, of taming horses in Flanders mud, of tricks of survival in the battlefield which scorned conventional heroism. He recounted these histories with stone-faced humour, with a cool self-knowing wryness, so that the surmounting of each of his life-and-death dilemmas sounded no more than a slick win at cards.

Now that he had returned at last from his mysterious wars he had taken up work as a forester, living in the depths of various local woods with a wife and four beautiful children. As he moved around, each cottage he settled in took on the same woody stamp of his calling, putting me in mind of charcoal-

231

burners and the lost forest-huts of Grimm. We boys loved to visit the Uncle Charles family, to track them down in the forest. The house would be wrapped in aromatic smoke, with winter logs piled in the yard, while from eaves and door-posts hung stoats'-tails, fox-skins, crow-bones, gin-traps and mice. In the kitchen there were axes and guns on the walls, a stone-jar of ginger in the corner, and on the mountainous fire a bubbling stew-pot of pigeon or perhaps a new-skinned hare.

There was some curious riddle about Uncle Charlie's early life which not even our Mother could explain. When the Boer War ended he had worked for a time in a Rand diamond town as a barman. Those were wide open days when a barman's duties included an ability to knock drunks cold. Uncle Charlie was obviously suited to this, for he was a lion of a man in his youth. The miners would descend from their sweating camps, pockets heavy with diamond dust, buy up barrels of whisky, drink themselves crazy, then start to burn down the saloon. . . . This was where Uncles Charles came in, the king-fish of those swilling bars, whose muscled bottle-swinging arm would then lay them out in rows. But even he was no superman and suffered his share of damage. The men used him

232

one night as a battering ram to break open a liquor store. He lay for two days with a broken skull, and still had a fine bump to prove it.

Then for two or three years he disappeared completely and went underground in the Johannesburg stews. No letters or news were received during that time, and what happened was never explained. Then suddenly, without warning, he turned up in Stroud, pale and thin and penniless. He wouldn't say where he'd been, or discuss what he'd done, but he'd finished his wanderings, he said. So a girl from our district, handsome Fanny Causon, took him and married him.

He settled then in the local forests and became one of the best woodsmen in the Cotswolds. His employers flattered, cherished and underpaid him; but he was content among his trees. He raised his family on labourer's pay, fed them on game from the woods, gave his daughters no discipline other than his humour, and taught his sons the skill of his heart.

It was a revelation of mystery to see him at work, somewhere in a cleared spread of the woods, handling seedlings like new-hatched birds, shaking out delicately their fibrous claws, and setting them firmly along the banks and hollows in the nests that his fingers had made. His gestures were caressive yet instinctive with power, and the plants settled ravenously to his touch, seemed to spread their small leaves with immediate life and to become rooted for ever where he left them.

The new woods rising in Horsley now, in Sheepscombe, in Rendcombe and Colne, are the forests my Uncle Charlie planted on thirty-five shillings a week. His are those mansions of summer shade, lifting skylines of leaves and birds, those blocks of new green now climbing our hills to restore their remembered perspectives. He died last year, and so did his wife—they died within a week of each other. But Uncle Charlie has left a mark on our landscape as permanent as he could wish.

*   *   *

The next of the Lights was Uncle Tom, a dark, quiet talker, full of hidden strength, who possessed a way with women. As I first remember him he was coachman-gardener at an old house in Woodchester. He was married by then to my Auntie Minnie—a tiny, pretty, parted-down-the-middle woman who resembled a Cruickshank drawing. Life in their small, neat stableyard—surrounded by potted ferns, high-stepping ponies and bright-painted traps and carriages—always seemed to me more toylike than human, and to visit them was to change one's scale and to leave the ponderous world behind.

Uncle Tom was well-mannered, something of a dandy, and he did peculiar things with his eyebrows. He could slide them independently up and down his forehead, and the habit was strangely suggestive. In moments of silence he did it constantly, as though to assure us he wished us well; and to this trick was ascribed much of his success with women—to this and to his dignified presence. As a bachelor he had suffered almost continuous pursuit; but though slow in manner he was fleet of foot and had given the girls a long run. Our Mother was proud of his successes. 'He was a cut above the usual,' she'd say. 'A proper gentleman. Just like King Edward. He thought nothing of spending a pound.'

When he was young, the girls died for him daily and bribed our Mother to plead their cause. They were always inviting her out to tea and things, and sending him messages, and ardent letters, wrapped up in bright scarves for herself. 'I was the most popular girl in the district,' she said. 'Our Tom was so refined. . . .'

For years Uncle Tom played a wily game and avoided entanglements. Then he met his match in Effie Mansell, a girl as ruthless as she was plain. According to Mother, Effie M was a monster, six foot high and as strong as a farm-horse. No sooner had she decided that she wanted Uncle Tom than she knocked him off his bicycle and told him. The very next morning he ran away to Worcester and took a job as a tram-conductor. He would have done far better to have gone down the mines, for the girl followed hot on his heels. She began to ride up and down all day long on his tram, where she had him at her mercy; and what made it worse, he had to pay her fares: he had never been so humiliated. In the end his nerve broke, he muddled the change, got the sack, and went to hide in a brick-quarry. But the danger passed, Effie married an inspector, and Uncle Tom returned to his horses.

By now he was chastened, and the stables reassured him—you could escape on a horse, not a tram. But what he wished for more than anything was a good woman's protection; he had found the pace too hot. So very soon after, he married the Minnie of his choice, abandoned his bachelor successes, and settled for good with a sigh of relief and a few astonishing runs on his eyebrows.

From then on Uncle Tom lived quietly and gratefully, like a prince in deliberate exile, merely dressing his face, from time to time, in those mantles of majesty and charm, those solemn winks and knowing convulsions of the brow which were all that remained of past grandeurs. . . .

★   ★   ★

My first encounter with Uncle Ray— prospector, dynamiter, buffalo-fighter, and builder of transcontinental railways—was an occasion of memorable suddenness. One moment he was a legend at the other end of the world, the next he was in my bed. Accustomed only to the satiny bodies of my younger brothers and sisters, I awoke one morning to find snoring beside me a huge and scaly man. I touched the thick legs and knotted arms and pondered the barbs on his chin, felt the crocodile flesh of this magnificent creature and wondered what it could be.

'It's your Uncle Ray come home,' whispered Mother. 'Get up now and let him sleep.'

I saw a rust-brown face, a gaunt Indian nose, and smelt a reek of cigars and train-oil.

Here was the hero of our school-boasting days, and to look on him was no disappointment. He was shiny as iron, worn as a rock, and lay like a chieftain sleeping. He'd come home on a visit from building his railways, loaded with money and thirst, and the days he spent at our house that time were full of wonder and conflagration.

For one thing he was unlike any other man we'd ever seen—or heard of, if it comes to that. With his leather-beaten face, wide teeth-crammed mouth, and far-seeing ice-blue eyes, he looked like some wigwam warrior stained with suns and heroic slaughter. He spoke the Canadian dialect of the railway camps in a drawl through his resonant nose. His body was tattooed in every quarter—ships in full sail, flags of all nations, reptiles and round-eyed maidens. By cunning flexings of his muscled flesh he could sail these ships, wave the flags in the wind, and coil snakes round the quivering girls.

Uncle Ray was a gift of the devil to us, a monstrous toy, a good-natured freak, more exotic than a circus ape. He would sit quite still while we examined him and absorb all our punishment. If we hit him he howled, if we pinched him he sobbed; he bore our aches and cramps like a Caliban. Or at a word he'd swing us round by our feet, or stand us upon his stomach, or lift us in pairs, one on either hand, and bump our heads on the ceiling.

But sooner or later he always said;

'Waal, boys, I gotta be going.'

He'd stand up and shake us off like fleas and start slowly to lick his lips.

'Where you got to go to, Uncle?'

'See a man 'bout a mule.'

'You ain't! Where you going? What for?'

'Get my fingers pressed. Tongue starched. Back oiled.'

'It ain't true! You're fibbing! Uncle . . .'

'Just *got* to, boys. See you all in the oven. Scrub yer elbows. Be good. So long.'

Off he'd go at a run; though the Lord knew where, *we* couldn't think of any place to go to. Then he'd come back much later, perhaps the following night, wet through, with a dog-like grin. He'd be unable to see properly, couldn't hang up his coat, couldn't find the latch on the door. He'd sit by the fire and steam and sing and flirt with the squawking girls. 'You'd best get to bed,' Mother would say severely; at which he'd burst into theatrical sobs. 'Annie, I can't! I can't move an inch. Got a bone in me leg . . . Mebbe two.'

One night, after he'd been missing for a couple of days, he came home on a bicycle, and rode it straight down the bank in the stormy darkness and crashed into the lavatory door. The girls ran out and fetched him indoors, howling and streaming with blood. They laid him full length on the kitchen table, then took off his boots and washed him. 'What a state he's in,' they giggled, shocked. 'It's whisky or something, Mother.' He began to sing, 'O, Dolly dear . . .' then started to eat the soap. He sang and blew bubbles, and we crowded around him, never having had any man in our house like this.

Word soon got round that Ray Light was home, laden with Canadian gold. He was set on by toughs, hunted by girls and warned several times by the police. He took most of this in his powerful stride, but the girls had him worried at times. A well-bred young seamstress whom he was cuddling in the picture-palace stole his dollar-crammed purse in the dark. Then one morning Beatie Burroughs arrived on our doorstep and announced that he'd promised to marry her. Under the Stroud Brewery arches, she said; just to clinch it. He had to hide for three days in our attic. . . .

But drunk or sober, Uncle Ray was the same; a great shaggy animal wagging off to his pleasures; a helpless giant, amiable, naïve,

sentimental and straightforwardly lustful. He
startled my sisters, but even so they adored
him; as for us boys, what more could we
want? He even taught us how to tie him up,
boasting that no knots could hold him. So we
tied him one night to a kitchen chair, watched
him struggle, and then went to bed. Mother
found him next morning on his hands and
knees, still tied up and fast asleep.

That visit of Uncle Ray's, with its games
and exhibitions, was like a prolonged
Christmas Day in the house. Routine, discipline and normal behaviour were suspended
during that time. We stayed up late, took
liberties, and shared his intoxications; while
he bounded about, disappeared on his
errands, returned in a tousled daze, fumbled
the girls, sang songs, fell down, got up and
handed dollars all round. Mother was prim by
turns and indulgent with him, either clicking
her tongue or giggling. And the girls were as
excited and assailed as we, though in a different, whispering way; saying Would you believe it? I never! How awful! or Did you hear
what he said to me then?

When he got through his money he went
back to Canada, back to the railway camps,
leaving behind him several broken heads,
fat innkeepers and well-set-up girls. Soon

after, while working in the snow-capped Rockies, he blew himself up with dynamite. He fell 90 feet down the Kicking Horse Pass and into a frozen lake. A Tamworth school-teacher—now my Auntie Elsie—travelled 4,000 miles to repair him. Having plucked him from the ice and thawed him out, she married him and brought him home. And that was the end of the pioneer days of that bounding prairie dog; without whom the Canadian Pacific Railway would never have reached the Pacific, at least, so we believe.

*   *   *

Moody, majestic Uncle Sid was the fourth, but not least of the brothers. This small powerful man, at first a champion cricketer, had a history blighted by rheumatism. He was a bus-driver too, after he left the Army, put in charge of our first double-deckers. Those solid-tyred, open-topped, passenger chariots were the leviathans of the roads at that time—staggering siege-towers which often ran wild and got their top-decks caught under bridges. Our Uncle Sid, one of the élite of the drivers, became a famous sight in the district. It was a thing of pride and some alarm to watch him go thundering by, perched up high in his reeking cabin, his face sweating beer and effort, while he wrenched and wrestled at the steering wheel to hold the great bus on its course. Each trip through the town destroyed roof-tiles and gutters and shook the gas mantles out of the lamps, but he always took pains to avoid women and children and scarcely ever mounted the pavements. Runaway roarer, freighted with human souls, stampeder of policemen and horses—it was Uncle Sid with his mighty hands who mastered its mad career.

Uncle Sid's story, like Uncle Charlie's, began in the South African War. As a private soldier he had earned a reputation for silence, cunning and strength. His talent for cricket, learned on the molehills of Sheepscombe, also endowed him with special privileges. Quite soon he was chosen to play for the Army and was being fed on the choicest rations. The hell-bent technique of his village game worked havoc among the officers. On a flat pitch at last, with a scorched dry wicket, after the hillocks and cow-dung of home, he was projected straightway into regions of greatness and broke records and nerves galore. His murderous bowling reduced heroes to panic; they just waved him good-bye and ran; and when he came in to bat men covered their heads and retired piecemeal to the boundaries. I can picture that squat little whizzing man knocking the cricket ball out of the ground, his face congested with brick-red fury, his shoulders bursting out of his braces. I can see him crouch for the next delivery, then spin on his short bowed legs, and clout it again half-way to Johannesburg while he heard far-off Sheepscombe cheer. In an old Transvaal newspaper, hoarded by Mother, I once found a scorecard which went something like this:

Army v. Transvaal. Pretoria 1899

ARMY

Col. 'Tigger' ffoukes-Wyte	1
Brig. Fletcher	0
Maj. T. W. G. Staggerton-Hake	12
Capt. V. O. Spillingham	0
Major Lyle (not)	31
Pte S. Light (not)	126
Extras	7
Total (for 4 dec.)	177

TRANSVAAL 21 all out (Pte S. Light 7 for 5)

This was probably the peak of Uncle Sid's glory, the time he would most wish to remember. From then on his tale shows a

244

certain fall—though it still flared up on occasions.

There was, for instance, the day of the Outing, when our village took three charabancs to Clevedon, with Uncle Sid driving the leading one, a crate of beer at his feet. 'Put her in top, Uncle Sid!' we cried, as we roared through the summer country. Guzzling with one hand, steering with the other, he drove through the flying winds, while we bounced and soared above the tops of the hedges, made airborne by this man at the wheel. . . .

Then on our way home, at the end of the day, we were stopped by a woman's screams. She stood by the roadside with a child in her arms, cringing from a threatening man. The tableau froze for us all to see: the wild-haired woman, the wailing child, the man with his arm upraised. Our charabancs came to a shuddering halt and we all started shouting at once. We leaned over the sides of our open wagons and berated the man for a scoundrel. Our men from their seats insulted him roundly, suggesting he leave the poor woman alone. But our Uncle Sid just folded his coat, climbed down from his cab without speaking, walked up to the bully, swung back his arm, and knocked the man straight through the hedge. Life to him was black and white and he had reacted to it simply. Scowling with pride, he returned to the wheel and drove us home a hero.

Uncle Sid differed in no way from his other brothers in chivalry, temper and drink. He could knock down a man or a glass of beer as readily and as neatly as they. But his job as a bus-driver (and his rheumatism) both increased—and obstructed—his thirst. The result exposed him to official censure, and it was here that the fates laid him low.

When he married my Aunt Alice, and became the father of two children, his job promised to anchor his wildness. But the law was against him and he soon got into scrapes. He was the best double-decker driver in Stroud, without doubt; even safer, more inspired when he drank. Everybody knew this—except the Bus Company. He began to get lectures, admonitions, stern warnings, and finally suspensions without pay.

When this last thing happened, out of respect for Aunt Alice, he always committed suicide. Indeed he committed suicide more than any man I know, but always in the most reasonable manner. If he drowned himself, then the canal was dry; if he jumped down a well, so was that; and when he drank disinfectant there was always an antidote ready,

246

clearly marked, to save everyone trouble. He reasoned, quite rightly, that Aunt Alice's anger, on hearing of another suspension, would be swallowed up by her larger anxiety on finding him again near to death. And Auntie Alice never failed him in this, and forgave him each time he recovered.

The Bus Company were almost equally forgiving; they took him back again and again. Then one night, having brought his bus safely home, they found him fast asleep at the wheel, reeking of malt and stone-jar cider; and they gave him the sack for good.

We were sitting in the kitchen rather late that night, when a loud knock came at the door. A hollow voice called 'Annie! Annie!' and we knew that something had happened. Then the kitchen door crept slowly open and revealed three dark-clad figures. It was Auntie Alice and her two small daughters, each dressed in their Sunday best. They stood at the foot of the kitchen steps, silent as apparitions, and Auntie Alice's face, with its huge drawn eyes, wore a mantle of tragic doom.

'He's done it this time,' she intoned at last. 'That's what. I know he has.'

Her voice had a churchlike incantation which dropped crystals of ice down my back.

She held the small pretty girls in a majestic embrace while they squirmed and sniffed and giggled.

'He never came home. They must have give him the sack. Now he's gone off to end it all.'

'No, no,' cried our Mother. 'Come and sit down, my dear.' And she drew her towards the fire.

Auntie Alice sat stiffly, like a Gothic image, still clutching her wriggling children.

'Where else could I go, Annie? He's gone down to Deadcombe. He always told me he would. . . .'

She suddenly turned and seized Mother's hands, her dark eyes rolling madly.

'Annie! Annie! He'll do himself in. Your boys—they just *got* to find him! . . .'

So Jack and I put on caps and coats and went out into the half-moon night. From so much emotion I felt light-headed; I wanted to laugh or hide. But Jack was his cool, intrepid self, tight-lipped as a gunboat commander. We were men in a crisis, on a secret mission, life and death seemed to hang on our hands. So we stuck close together and trudged up the valley, heading for Deadcombe Wood.

The wood was a waste of rotting silence, transformed by its mask of midnight; a fine rain was falling, wet ferns soaked our legs, leaves shuddered with owls and water. What were we supposed to do? we wondered. Why had we come, anyway? We beat up and down through the dripping trees, calling 'Uncle!' in chill, flat voices. What should we find? Perhaps nothing at all. Or worse, what we had come to seek. . . . But we remembered the women, waiting fearfully at home. Our duty, though dismal, was clear.

So we stumbled and splashed through invisible brooks, followed paths, skirted ominous shadows. We poked bits of stick into piles of old leaves, prodded foxholes, searched the length of the wood. There was nothing there but the fungoid darkness, nothing at all but our fear.

We were about to go home, and gladly enough, when suddenly we saw him. He was standing tiptoe under a great dead oak with his braces around his neck. The elastic noose, looped to the branch above him, made him bob up and down like a puppet. We approached the contorted figure with dread; saw his baleful eye fixed on us.

Our Uncle Sid was in a terrible temper.

'You've been a bloody long time!' he said.

*   *   *

Uncle Sid never drove any buses again but took a job as a gardener in Sheepscombe. All the uncles now, from their wilder beginnings, had resettled their roots near home—all, that is, save Insurance Fred, whom we lost through prosperity and distance. These men reflected many of Mother's qualities, were foolish, fantastical, moody; but in spite of their follies they remained for me the true heroes of my early life. I think of them still in the image they gave me; they were bards and oracles each; like a ring of squat megaliths on some local hill, bruised by weather and scarred with old glories. They were the horsemen and brawlers of another age, and their lives spoke its long farewell. Spoke too, of campaigns on desert marches, of Kruger's cannon and Flanders mud; of a world that still moved at the same pace as Caesar's, and of that Empire greater than his—through which they had fought, sharp-eyed and anonymous, and seen the first outposts crumble. . . .

OUTINGS AND FESTIVALS

THE year revolved around the village, the festivals round the year, the Church round the festivals, the Squire round the Church, and the village round the Squire. The Squire was our centre, a crumbling moot tree; and few indeed of our local celebrations could take place without his shade. On the greater occasions he let us loose in his gardens, on the smaller gave us buns and speeches; and at historic moments of national rejoicing—when kings were born, enemies vanquished, or the Conservatives won an election—he ransacked his box-rooms for fancy-dresses that we might rejoice in a proper manner.

The first big festival that I can remember was Peace Day in 1919. It was a day of magical transformations, of tears and dusty sunlight, of bands, processions, and buns by the cartload; and I was so young I thought it normal. . . .

We had all been provided with fancy-dress, and that seemed normal too. Apart from the Squire's contribution Marjorie had been busy for weeks stitching up glories for ourselves and the neighbours. No makeshift, rag-bag

251

cobbling either; Marjorie had worked as though for a wedding.

On the morning of the feast Poppy Green came to the house to try on her angel's dress. She was five years old and about my size. She had russet curls like apple peelings, a polished pumpkin face, a fruity air of exploding puddings, and a perpetual cheeky squint. I loved her, she was like a portable sweet-shop. This morning I watched my sisters dress her. She was supposed to represent a spirit. They'd made her a short frilly frock, a tinfoil helmet, cardboard wings, and a wand with a star. When they'd clothed her they stood her up on the mantelpiece and had a good look at her. Then they went off awhile on some other business and left us alone together.

'Fly!' I commanded. 'You got wings, ain't you?'

Poppy squirmed and wiggled her shoulders.

I grew impatient and pushed her off the mantelpiece, and she fell with a howl into the fireplace. Looking down at her, smudged with coal and tears, her wand and wings all crumpled, I felt nothing but rage and astonishment. She should have been fluttering round the room.

They sponged and soothed her, and Poppy

trotted home, her bent wand clutched in her hand. Then shapes and phantoms began to run through the village, and we started to get ready ourselves. Marge appeared as Queen Elizabeth, with Phyllis her lady-in-waiting. Marjorie, who was sixteen and at her most beautiful, wore a gown of ermine, a brocaded bodice, and a black cap studded with pearls. She filled the kitchen with such a glow of grace that we just stood and gaped at her. It was the first time I had seen Queen Elizabeth, but this was no sharp-faced Tudor. Tender and proud in her majestic robes, she was the Queen of Heaven, risen from the dust, unrecognizable as Marge till she spoke, and her eyes shone down on us from her veils of ermine like emeralds laid in snow. Thirteen-year-old Phyllis, with finery of her own, skipped like a magpie around her, wearing a long chequered dress of black and white velvet, and a hat full of feathers and moths.

The rest of us, whom Marjorie had dressed, were the result of homespun inspirations. Dorothy, as 'Night', was perhaps the most arresting; an apparition of unearthly beauty, a flash of darkness, a strip of nocturnal sky, mysteriously cloaked in veils of black netting entangled with silver paper. A crescent moon lay across her breast, a comet across her brow, and her long dark curls fell in coils of midnight and were sprinkled with tinsel dust. I smelt frost when I saw her and heard a crackling of stars; familiar Dorothy had grown far and disturbing.

Brother Jack had refused to be dressed up at all, unless in some aspect of recognized valour. So they hung him in green, gave him a bow and arrow, and he called himself Robin Hood. Little Tony was dressed as a market-girl, curly-headed and pretty as love, bare-armed and bonneted, carrying a basket of flowers, but so proud we forgave him his frock.

As for me, a squat neck and solid carriage made the part I should play inevitable. I was John Bull—whoever he was—but I quickly surmised his importance. I remember the girls stuffing me into my clothes with many odd squeals and giggles. Gravely I offered an arm or leg, but remained dignified and aloof. Marjorie had assembled the ritual garments with her usual flair and cunning. I wore a top-hat and choker, a union-jack waistcoat, a frock-coat, and pillowcase britches. But I'd been finished off hurriedly with gaiters of cardboard fastened loosely together with pins—a slovenly makeshift which offended my taste, and which I was never able to forgive.

This Peace Day I remember as a blur of colour, leading from fury to triumph. There was a procession with a band. I walked alone solemnly. Fantastic disguises surrounded me; every single person seemed covered with beards, false-noses, bootblack and wigs. We had not marched far when my boots fell off, followed by my cardboard gaiters. As I stopped to find them, the procession swept over me. I sat down by the roadside and howled. I howled because I could hear the band disappearing, because I was John Bull and it should not have happened. I was picked up by a carriage, restored to the procession, then placed on a trolley and pulled. Cross-legged on the trolley, bare-footed and gaiter-less, I rode like a prince through the village.

Dusty, sweating from its long route-march, the procession snaked round the houses. The old and infirm stood and cheered from the gutters; I nodded back from my trolley. At last we entered the cool beech wood through which the Squire's drive twisted. The brass-band's thunder bounced back from the boughs. Owls hooted and flapped away.

We came out of the wood into the Big House gardens, and the sun returned in strength. Doves and pigeons flew out of the cedars. The swans took off from the lake. On

255

the steps of the Manor stood the wet-eyed Squire, already in tears at the sight of us. His mother, in a speech from a basket-chair, mentioned the glory of God, the Empire, us; and said we wasn't to touch the flowers.

With that the procession dispersed, I was tipped off the trolley, and I wandered away through the grounds. Flags and roses moved against the sky, bright figures among the bushes. Japanese girls and soot-faced savages grew strangely from banks of lilac. I saw Charlie Chaplin, Peter the Pieman, a collection of upright tigers, a wounded soldier about my age, and a bride on the arm of a monkey.

Later I was given a prize by the Squire and was photographed in a group by a rockery. I still have that picture, all sepia shadows, a leaf ripped from that summer day. Surrounded by girls in butter muslin, by druids and eastern kings, I am a figure rooted in unshakable confidence, oval, substantial and proud. About two feet high and two feet broad, my britches like slack balloons, I stand, top-hatted, with a tilted face as severe as on a Roman coin. Others I recognize are gathered round me, all marked by that day's white dust. Tony has lost his basket of flowers, Jack his bow and arrow. Poppy

Green has had her wings torn off and is grasping a broken lily. She stands beside me, squinting fiercely, ruffled a bit by the heat, and the silver letters across her helmet—which I couldn't read then—say PEACE.

*   *   *

Our village outings were both sacred and secular, and were also far between. One seldom, in those days, strayed beyond the parish boundaries, except for the annual Choir Outing. In the meantime we had our own tribal wanderings, unsanctified though they were, when a sudden fine morning would send us forth in families for a day's nutting or blackberrying. So up we'd go to the wilder end of the valley, to the bramble-entangled Scrubs, bearing baskets and buckets and flasks of cold tea, like a file of foraging Indians. Blackberries clustered against the sky, heavy and dark as thunder, which we plucked and gobbled, hour after hour, lips purple, hands stained to the wrists. Or later, mushrooms, appearing like manna, buttoning the shaggy grass, found in the mists of September mornings with the wet threads of spiders on them. They came in the night from nowhere, rootless, like a scattering of rubber balls. Their suckers clung to the roots of grass and broke off with a rubbery snap. The skin rubbed away like the bark of a birch tree, the flesh tasted of something unknown. . . . At other times there would be wild green damsons, tiny plums, black sloes, pink crab-apples—the free waste of the woods, an unpoliced bounty, which we'd carry back home in bucketfuls. Whether we used them for jam or jellies or pies, or just left them to rot, didn't matter.

Then sometimes there'd be a whole day's outing, perhaps to Sheepscombe to visit relations—a four-mile walk, which to our short legs seemed further, so that we needed all day to do it. We would start out early, with the sun just rising and the valley wrapped in mist. . . .

'It's going to be hot,' says our Mother brightly, and usually she is right. We climb up slowly towards Bulls Cross, picking at the bushes for birds'-nests. Or we stop to dig holes or to swing on gates while Mother looks back at the view. 'What a picture,' she murmurs. 'Green as green. . . . And those poppies, red as red.' The mist drags the tree-tops, flies away in the sky, and there is suddenly blue air all round us.

Painswick sprawls white in the other

valley, like the skeleton of a foundered mammoth. But active sounds of its working morning—carts and buzz-saws, shouts and hammering—come drifting in gusts towards us. The narrow lane that leads to Sheepscombe bends steeply away on our right. 'Step out, young men!' our Mother says crisply. She begins to teach us a hymn; the kind that cries for some lost land of paradise, and goes well with a tambourine. I've not heard it before (nor ever since), but it entirely enshrines our outing—the remote, shaggy valley in which we find ourselves, the smell of hot straw on the air, dog-roses and distances, dust and spring waters, and the long day's journey, by easy stages, to the sheep-folds of our wild relations.

They are waiting for us with warm ginger-beer, and a dinner of broad beans and bacon. Aunty Fan says, 'Annie, come in out of the sun. You must be ready to drop.' We go indoors and find our Uncle Charlie hacking at the bacon with a bill-hook. Young cousin Edie and her cautious brothers seem to be pondering whether to punch our heads. Our Gramp comes in from his cottage next door, dressed in mould-green corduroy suiting. We sit down and eat, and the cousins kick us under the table, from excitement rather than spite.

Then we play with their ferrets, spit down their well, have a fight, and break down a wall. Later we are called for and given a beating, then we climb up the tree by the earth closet. Edie climbs highest, till we bite her legs, then she hangs upside down and screams. It has been a full, far-flung and satisfactory day; dusk falls, and we say good-bye.

Back down the lane in the thick hot darkness we walk drowsily, heavy with boots. Night odours come drifting from woods and gardens; sweet musks and sharp green acids. In the sky the fat stars bounce up and down, rhythmically, as we trudge along. Glowworms, brighter than lamps or candles, spike the fields with their lemon fires, while huge horned beetles stumble out of the dark and buzz blindly around our heads.

Then Painswick appears—a starfish of light dilating in a pool of distance. We hurry across the haunted common and come at last to the top of our valley. The village waterfall, still a mile away, lifts its cool, familiar murmur. We are nearing home, we are almost there: Mother starts to recite a poem. 'I remember, I remember, the house where I was born. . .' She says it right through, and I tag beside her watching the trees walk past in the sky. . . .

The first Choir Outing we ever had was a jaunt in a farm-wagon to Gloucester. Only the tenors and basses and the treble boys were included in that particular treat. Later, with the coming of the horse-brake and charabanc, the whole village took part as well. With the help of the powerful new charabanc we even got out of the district altogether, rattling away to the ends of the earth, to Bristol or even further.

One year the Outing was to Weston-super-Mare, and we had saved up for months to be worthy of it. We spent the night before preparing our linen, and the girls got up at dawn to make sandwiches. The first thing I did when I came down that morning was to go out and look at the weather. The sky was black, and Tony was behind the lavatory praying hard through his folded hands. When he saw that I'd seen him he began to scratch and whistle, but the whole thing was a very bad sign.

We couldn't eat breakfast, the porridge was like gravel; so Jack and I ran up the bank to see what was going on. Families were already gathering for the charabancs, so we ran back

261

down again. The girls were ready, and Tony was ready. Mother was raking under the piano with a broomstick.

'Come on, our Mother! They'll go without us!'

'I've just got to find my corsets.'

She found them; then started very slowly to wash, like a duck with all summer to do it. We stood round and nagged her, rigid with nerves.

'Run along—you're under my feet.'

So we left her, and scampered along to the Woolpack. The whole village was waiting by now; mothers with pig-buckets stuffed with picnics, children with cocoa-tin spades, fathers with bulging overcoats lined entirely with clinking bottles. There was little Mrs Tulley collecting the fares and plucking at her nervous cheeks; Mr Vick, the shopkeeper, carrying his keys in a basket; the two dress-makers in unclaimed gowns; and Lily Nelson, a fugitive from her brother, whispering, 'You mustn't tell Arnold—he'd kill me.' The Squire's old gardener had brought a basket of pigeons which he planned to release from the pier. And the postman, having nobody to deliver his letters to, had dumped them, and was coming along too.

Faces looked pale in the early light. Men

sniffed and peered at the sky. 'Don't look too good, do it?' 'Can't say it do.' 'Bloody black over Stroud.' 'Might clear though. . . .' Teeth were sucked in, heads doubtfully shaken; I felt the doom of storm-sickness on me.

The vicar arrived to see us off—his pyjamas peeping out from his raincoat. 'There's a very nice church near the Promenade. . . . I trust you will all spare a moment. . . .' He issued each choirboy with his shilling for dinner, then dodged back home to bed. The last to turn up was Herbert the gravedigger, with something queer in a sack. The last, that is, except our Mother, of whom there was still no sign.

Then the charabancs arrived and everyone clambered aboard, fighting each other for seats. We abandoned our Mother and climbed aboard too, feeling guilty and miserable. The charabancs were high, with broad open seats and with folded tarpaulins at the rear, upon which, as choirboys, we were privileged to perch and to fall off and break our necks. We all took our places, people wrapped themselves in blankets, horns sounded, and we were ready. 'Is everyone present?' piped the choirmaster. Shamefully, Jack and I kept silent.

Our Mother, as usual, appeared at that

moment, a distant trotting figure, calling and waving her handbags gaily to disarm what impatience there might be. 'Come on, Mother Lee! We near went without you!' Beaming, she climbed aboard. 'I just had to wash out my scarf,' she said, and tied it on the windscreen to dry. And there it blew like a streaming pennant as we finally drove out of the village.

In our file of five charabancs, a charioted army, we swept down the thundering hills. At the speed and height of our vehicles the whole valley took on new dimensions; woods rushed beneath us, and fields and flies were devoured in a gulp of air. We were windborne now by motion and pride, we cheered everything, beast and fowl, and taunted with heavy ironical shouts those unfortunates still working in the fields. We kept this up till we had roared through Stroud, then we entered the stranger's country. It was no longer so easy to impress pedestrians that we were the Annual Slad Choir Outing. So we settled down, and opened our sandwiches, and began to criticize the farming we passed through.

The flatness of the Severn Valley now seemed dull after our swooping hills, the salmon-red sandstone of the Clifton Gorges too florid compared with our chalk. Every-thing began to appear strange and comic, we hooted at the shapes of the hayricks, laughed at the pitiful condition of the cattle—'He won't last long—just look at 'is knees.' We began to look round fondly at our familiar selves, drawn close by this alien country. Waves of affection and loyalty embraced us. We started shouting across the seats. 'Harry! Hey, Harry! Say, whatcher, Harry! Bit of all right, ain't it, you? Hey, Bert! 'Ow's Bert? 'Ow you doin' ole sparrer? Where's Walt? Hey there, Walt! Watcher!'

Mile after rattling mile we went, under the racing sky, flying neckties and paper kites from the back, eyes screwed in the weeping wind. The elders, protected in front by the windscreen, chewed strips of bacon, or slept. Mother pointed out landmarks and lectured the sleepers on points of historical interest. Then a crawling boy found the basket of pigeons and the coach exploded with screams and wings. . . . .

The weather cleared as we drove into Weston, and we halted on the Promenade, 'The seaside,' they said: we gazed around us, but saw no sign of the sea. We saw a vast blue sky and an infinity of mud stretching away to the shadows of Wales. But rousing smells of

265

an invisible ocean astonished our land-locked nostrils: salt, and wet weeds, and fishy oozes; a sharp difference in every breath. Our deep-ditched valley had not prepared us for this, for we had never seen such openness, the blue windy world seemed to have blown quite flat, bringing the sky to the level of our eyebrows. Canvas booths flapped on the edge of the Prom, mouths crammed with shellfish and vinegar; there were rows of prim boarding-houses (each the size of our Vicarage); bath-chairs, carriages and donkeys; and stilted far out on the rippled mud a white pier like a sleeping dragon.

The blue day was ours; we rattled our money and divided up into groups. 'Hey, Jake, Steve; let's go have a wet'—and the men shuffled off down a side street. 'I'm beat after that, Mrs Jones, ain't you?—there's a clean place down by the bandstand.' The old women nodded, and went seeking their comforts; the young ones to stare at the police-men.

Meanwhile, we boys just picked up and ran; we had a world of mud to deal with. The shops and streets ended suddenly, a frontier to the works of man; and beyond—the mud, salt winds and birds, a kind of double ration of light, a breathless space neither fenced nor claimed, and far out a horizon of water. We whinnied like horses and charged up and down, every hoof-mark written behind us. If you stamped in this mud, you brought it alive, the footprint began to speak, it sucked and sighed and filled with water, became a foot cut out of the sky. I dug my fingers into a stretch of mud to see how deep it was, felt a hard flat pebble and drew it out and examined it in the palm of my hand. Suddenly, it cracked, and put out two claws; I dropped it in horror, and ran. . .

Half the village now had hired themselves chairs and were bravely facing the wind. Mrs Jones was complaining about Weston tea: 'It's made from the drains, I reckon.' The Squire's old gardener, having lost his pigeons, was trying to catch gulls in a basket; and the gravedigger (who appeared to have brought his spade) was out on the mud digging holes. Then the tide came in like a thick red sludge, and we all went on the pier.

Magic construction striding the waves, loaded with freaks and fancies, water-shutes and crumpled mirrors, and a whole series of nightmares for a penny. One glided secretly to one's favourite machine, the hot coin burning one's hand, to command a murder, a drunk's delirium, a haunted grave or a Newgate hanging. This last, of course, was my favourite; what dread power one's penny purchased—the painted gallows, the nodding priest, the felon with his face of doom. At a touch they jerked through their ghastly dance, the priest, the hangman and the convict, joined together by rods and each one condemned as it were to perpetual torment. Their ritual motions led to the jerk of the corpse; the figures froze and the lights went out. Another penny restored the lights, brought back life to the cataleptic trio, and dragged the poor felon once more to the gallows to be strangled all over again.

That white pier shining upon the waves seemed a festive charnel house. With our mouths hanging open, sucking gory sticks of rock, we groped hungrily from horror to horror. For there were sideshows too, as well as the machines, with hair-raising freaks under glass—including a two-headed Indian, a seven-legged sheep, and a girl's eye with a child coiled inside it.

We spent more time on that turgid pier than anywhere else in Weston. Then the tide went out, and evening fell, and we returned to the waiting charabancs. People came wandering from all directions, with bags full of whelks and seaweed, the gravedigger was dragged from his holes in the sand, and our numbers were checked and counted. Then we were all in our seats, the tarpaulin pulled over us, and with a blast of horns we left.

A long homeward drive through the red of twilight, through landscapes already relinquished, the engines humming, the small children sleeping, and the young girls gobbling shrimps. At sunset we stopped at a gaslit pub for the men to have one more drink. This lasted till all of them turned bright pink and started embracing their wives. Then we repacked the charabancs, everyone grew drowsy, and we drove through the darkness beyond Bristol. The last home stretch: someone played a harmonica; we boys groped for women to sleep on, and slept, to the sway and sad roar of the coach and the men's thick boozy singing.

We passed Stroud at last and climbed the valley road, whose every curve our bodies recognized, whose every slant we leaned to, though still half asleep, till we woke to the smell of our houses. We were home, met by lanterns—and the Outing was over. With subdued 'Good-nights' we collected into families, then separated towards our beds. Where soon I lay, my head ringing with sleep, my ears full of motors and organs, my shut eyes printed with the images of the day— mud, and red rock, and hangmen. . . .

* * *

The Parochial Church Tea and Annual Entertainment was the village's winter treat. It took place in the school-room, round about Twelfth Night, and cost us a shilling to go. The Tea was an orgy of communal gluttony, in which everyone took pains to eat more than his money's worth and the helpers ate more than the customers. The Entertainment which followed, home-produced and by lamp-light, provided us with sufficient catch phrases for a year.

Regularly, for a few weeks before the night, one witnessed the same scenes in our kitchen, the sisters sitting in various corners of the room, muttering secretly to themselves, smiling, nodding and making lah-di-dah gestures with a kind of intent and solitary madness. They were rehearsing their sketches for the Entertainment, which I found impossible not to learn too, so that I would be haunted for days by three nightmare monologues full of one-sided unanswered questions.

On the morning of the Feast we got the

school ready. We built a stage out of trestles and planks. Mr Robinson was in the cloakroom slicing boiled ham, where he'd been for the last three days, and three giggling helpers were now forking the meat and slapping it into sandwiches. Outside in the yard John Barraclough had arrived and set up his old field kitchen, had broken six hurdles across his knee and filled up the boiler with water. Laid out on the wall were thirty-five teapots, freshly washed and drying in the wind. The feast was preparing; and by carrying chairs, helping with the stage, and fetching water from the spring, Jack and I made ourselves sufficiently noticeable to earn a free ticket each.

Punctually at six, with big eating to be done, we returned to the lighted school. Villagers with lanterns streamed in from all quarters. We heard the bubbling of water in Barraclough's boiler, smelt the sweet wood smoke from his fire, saw his red face lit like a turnip lamp as he crouched to stoke up the flames.

We lined up in the cold, not noticing the cold, waiting for the doors to open. When they did, it was chins and boots and elbows, no queues, we just fought our way in. Lamplight and decorations had transformed the schoolroom from a prison into a banqueting hall. The long trestle-tables were patterned with food; fly-cake, brown buns, ham-sandwiches. The two stoves were roaring, reeking of coke. The helpers had their teapots charged. We sat down stiffly and gazed at the food; fidgeted, coughed and waited. . .

The stage-curtains parted to reveal the Squire, wearing a cloak and a deer-stalking hat. He cast his dim, wet eyes round the crowded room, then sighed and turned to go. Somebody whispered from behind the curtain; 'Bless me!' said the Squire, and came back.

'The Parochial Church Tea!' he began, then paused. 'Is with us again. . . . I suggest. And Entertainment. Another year! Another year comes round! . . . When I see you all gathered together here—once more—when I see—when I think. . . . And here you all are! When I see you here—as I'm sure you all are—once again. . . . It comes to me, friends!—how time—how you—how all of us here—as it were. . . .' His moustache was quivering, tears ran down his face, he groped for the curtains and left.

His place was taken by the snow-haired vicar, who beamed weakly upon us all.

'What is the smallest room in the world?' he

asked.

'A mushroom!' we bawled, without hesitation.

'And the largest, may I ask?'

'ROOM FOR IMPROVEMENT!'

'You know it,' he muttered crossly. Recovering himself, he folded his hands: 'And now O bountiful Father . . .'

We barked through grace and got our hands on the food and began to eat it any old order. Cakes, buns, ham, it didn't matter at all, we just worked from one plate to the next. Folk by the fires fanned themselves with sandwiches, a joker fried ham on the stove, steaming brown teapots passed up and down, and we were so busy there was small conversation. Through the lighted windows we could see snow falling, huge feathers against the dark. 'It's old Mother Hawkins a-plucking her geese!' cried someone; an excellent omen. Twelfth Night, and old Mother Hawkins at work, up in the sky with her birds; we loosened our belts and began to nod at each other; it was going to be a year of fat.

We had littered the tables with our messy leavings of cake-crumbs and broken meat; some hands still went through the motions of eating, but clearly we'd had enough. The vicar rose to his feet again, and again we thanked the Lord. 'And now, my friends, comes the—er—feast for the soul. If you would care to—ah—take the air a moment, willing hands are waiting to clear the hall and prepare for the—um—Entertainment. . . .'

We crowded outside and huddled in the snow while the tables were taken away. Inside, behind curtains, the actors were making up—and my moment, too, was approaching. The snow whirled about me and I began to sweat, I wanted to run off home. Then the doors reopened and I crouched by the stove, shivering and chattering with nerves. The curtains parted and the Entertainment began with a comic I neither saw nor heard. . . .

'For the next item, ladies and gentlemen, we have an instrumental duet, by Miss Brown and—er—young Laurie Lee.'

Smirking with misery I walked to the stage. Eileen's face was as white as a minim. She sat at the piano, placed the music crooked, I straightened it, it fell to the ground. I groped to retrieve it; we looked at one another with hatred; the audience was still as death. Eileen tried to give me an A, but struck B instead, and I tuned up like an ape threading needles. At last we were ready, I raised my fiddle; and Eileen was off like a bolting horse. I caught her up in the middle of the piece—which I believe was a lullaby—and after playing the repeats, only twice as fast, we just stopped, frozen motionless, spent.

Some hearty stamping and whistling followed, and a shout of 'Give us another!' Eileen and I didn't exchange a glance, but we loved each other now. We found the music of 'Danny Boy' and began to give it all our emotion, dawdling dreamily among the fruitier chords and scampering over the high bits; till the audience joined in, using their hymn-singing voices, which showed us the utmost respect. When it was over I returned to my seat by the stove, my body feeling smooth and beautiful. Eileen's mother was weeping into her hat, and so was mine, I think. . . .

Now I was free to become one of the audience, and the Entertainment burgeoned before me. What had seemed to me earlier as the capering of demons now became a spectacle of human genius. Turn followed turn in variety and splendour. Mr Crosby, the organist, told jokes and stories as though his very life depended on them, trembling, sweating, never pausing for a laugh, and rolling his eyes at the wings for rescue. We loved him, however, and wouldn't let him go, while he grew more and more hysterical, racing through monologues, gabbling songs about shrimps, skipping, mopping, and jumping up and down, as though humouring a tribe of savages.

Major Doveton came next, with his Indian banjo, which was even harder to tune than my fiddle. He straddled a chair and began wrestling with the keys, cursing us in English and Urdu. Then all the strings broke, and he snarled óff the stage and started kicking the banjo round the cloakroom. He was followed by a play in which Marjorie, as Cinderella, sat in a goose-feathered dress in a castle. While waiting for the pumpkin to turn into a coach, she sang 'All alone by the telephone'.

Two ballads came next, and Mrs Pimbury, a widow, sang them both with astonishing spirit. The first invited us to go with her to Canada; the second was addressed to a mushroom:

> *Grow! Grow! Grow little mushroom grow!*
> *Somebody wants you soon.*
> *I'll call again tomorrow morning—*
>   *See!*
> *And if you've growen bigger you will just*
>   *suit ME!*
> *So Grow! Grow! Grow little mushroom—*
>   *Grow!*

Though we'd not heard this before, it soon became part of our heritage, as did the song of a later lady. This last—the Baroness von Hodenburg—sealed our entertainment with almost professional distinction. She was a guest star from Sheepscombe and her appearance was striking, it enshrined all the mystery of art. She wore a loose green gown like a hospital patient's, and her hair was red and long. 'She writes,' whispered Mother. 'Poems and booklets and that.'

'I am going to sink you,' announced the lady, 'a little ditty I convected myself. Bose vords und music, I may say, is mine—und zey refer to ziss pleasant valleys.'

With that she sat down, arched her beautiful back, raised her bangled wrists over the keyboard, then ripped off some startling runs and trills, and sang with a ringing laugh:

Elfin volk come over the hill!
Come und dance, just vere you vill!
Brink your pipes, und brink your flutes,
Brink your sveetly soundink notes!
Come avay-hay! Life is gay-hay!
Life—Is—Gay!

We thought this song soppy, but we never

forgot it. From then on, whenever we saw the Baroness in the lanes we used to bawl the song at her through the hedges. But she would only stop, and cock her head, and smile dreamily to herself. . . .

After these songs the night ended with slapstick; rough stuff about babies, chaps dressed as women, broad Gloucester exchanges between yokels and toffs, with the yokels coming off best. We ached with joy, and kicked at the chairs; but we knew the end was coming. The vicar got up, proposed a vote of thanks, and said oranges would be distributed at the gate. The National Anthem was romped through, we all began coughing, then streamed outdoor through the snow.

Back home our sisters discussed their performances till the tears dripped off their noses. But to us boys it was not over, not till tomorrow; there was still one squeeze left in the lemon. Tomorrow, very early, we'd go back to the school-room, find the baskets of broken food—half-eaten buns, ham coated with cake-crumbs—and together we'd finish the lot.

FIRST BITE AT THE APPLE

So quiet was Jo always, so timorous yet eager to please, that she was the one I chose first. There were others, of course, louder and more bouncingly helpful, but it was Jo's cool face, tidy brushed-back hair, thin body and speechless grace which provided the secretive prettiness I needed. Unknowingly, therefore, she became the pathfinder, the slender taper I carried to the grottoes in whose shadows I now found myself wandering.

I used to seek her out on her way home from school, slyly separate her from the others, watch her brass bracelet dangling. Was I eleven or twelve? I don't know—she was younger. She smiled easily at me from the gutter.

'Where you going then, Jo?'

'Nowhere special.'

'Oh.'

It was all right so long as she didn't move.

'Let's go down the bank then. Shall us? Eh?'

No answer, but no attempt to escape.

'Down the bank. Like before. How about

279

it, Jo?'

Still no answer, no sign or look. She didn't even stop the turning of her bracelet, but she came down the bank all the same. Stepping toe-pointed over the ant-heaps, walking straight and near and silent, she showed no knowledge of what she was going for, only that she was going with me.

Close under the yews, in the heavy green evening, we sat ourselves solemnly down. The old red trees threw arches above us, making tunnels of rusty darkness. Jo, like a slip of yew, was motionless; she neither looked at me nor away. I leant on one elbow and tossed a stone into the trees, heard it skipping from branch to branch.

'What shall we do then, Jo?' I asked.

She made no reply, as usual.

'What d'you say, Jo?'

'I don't mind.'

'Come on—you tell.'

'No, you.'

The pronouncement had always to come from me. She waited to hear me say it. She waited, head still, staring straight before her, tugging gently at a root of weed.

'Good-morning, Mrs Jenkins!' I said breezily. 'What seems to be the trouble?'

Without a blink or a word Jo lay down on

the grass and gazed up at the red-berried yews, stretched herself subtly on her green crushed bed, and scratched her calf, and waited. The game was formal and grave in character, its ritual rigidly patterned. Silent as she lay, my hands moved as silently, and even the birds stopped singing.

Her body was pale and milk-green on the grass, like a birch-leaf lying in water, slightly curved like a leaf and veined and glowing, lit faintly from within its flesh. This was not Jo now but the revealed unknown, a labyrinth of naked stalks, stranger than flesh, smoother than candleskins, like something thrown down from the moon. Time passed, and the cool limbs never moved, neither towards me nor yet away; she just turned a grass ring around her fingers and stared blindly away from my eyes. The sun fell slanting and struck the spear-tipped grass, laying tiger-stripes round her hollows, binding her body with crimson bars, and moving slow colours across her.

Night and home seemed far away. We were caught in the rooted trees. Knees wet with dew I pondered in silence all that Jo's acquiescence taught me. She shivered slightly and stirred her hands. A blackbird screamed into a bush. . . .

'Well, that'll be all, Mrs Jenkins,' I said. 'I'll be back again tomorrow.'

I rose from my knees, mounted an invisible horse, and cantered away to supper. While Jo dressed quietly and dawdled home, alone among the separate trees.

*   *   *

Of course, they discovered us in the end; we must have thought we were invisible. 'What about it, young lad? You and Jo—last night? Ho, yes! we seen you, arf! arf!' A couple of cowmen had stopped me in the road; I denied it, but I wasn't surprised. Sooner or later one was always caught out, but the thing was as readily forgotten; very little in the village was either secret or shocking, we merely repeated ourselves. Such early sex-games were formal exercises, a hornless charging of calves; but we were certainly lucky to live in a village, the landscape abounded with natural instruction which we imitated as best we could; if anyone saw us they laughed their heads off—and there were no magistrates to define us obscene.

This advantage was shared by young and old, was something no town can know. We knew ourselves to be as corrupt as any other community of our size—as any London street, for instance. But there was no tale-bearing then or ringing up 999; transgressors were dealt with by local opinion, by silence, lampoons or nicknames. What we were spared from seeing—because the village protected itself—were the crimes of our flesh written cold in a charge sheet, the shady arrest, the police-court autopsy, the headline of magistrate's homilies.

As for us boys, it is certain that most of us, at some stage or other of our growth, would have been rounded up under present law, and quite a few shoved into reform school. Instead we emerged—culpable it's true—but unclassified in criminal record. No wilder or milder than Battersea boys, we were less ensnared by bye-laws. If caught in the act, we got a quick bashing; and the fist of the farmer we'd robbed of apples or eggs seemed more natural and just than any cold-mouthed copper adding one more statistic for the book. It is not crime that has increased, but its definition. The modern city, for youth, is a police-trap.

Our village was clearly no pagan paradise, neither were we conscious of showing tolerance. It was just the way of it. We certainly committed our share of statutory crime.

Manslaughter, arson, robbery, rape cropped up regularly throughout the years. Quiet incest flourished where the roads were bad; some found their comfort in beasts; and there were the usual friendships between men and boys who walked through the fields like lovers. Drink, animality and rustic boredom were responsible for most. The village neither approved nor disapproved, but neither did it complain to authority. Sometimes our sinners were given hell, taunted and pilloried, but their crimes were absorbed in the local scene and their punishment confined to the parish.

★   ★   ★

So when, in due time, I breathed the first faint musks of sex, my problem was not one of guilt or concealment but of simple revelation. That early exploration of Jo's spread body was a solitary studying of maps. The signs upon her showed the way I should go, then she was folded and put away. Very soon I caught up with other travellers, all going in the same direction. They received me naturally, the boys and girls of my age, and together we entered the tricky wood. Daylight and an easy lack of shame illuminated our actions. Banks and brakes were our tiring houses, and curiosity our first concern. We were awkward, convulsed, but never surreptitious, being protected by our long knowledge of each other. And we were all of that green age which could do no wrong, so unformed as yet and coldly innocent we did little more than mime the realities.

The girls played their part of invitation and show, and were rather more assured than we were. They sensed they had come into their own at last. For suddenly they were not creatures to order about any more, not the makeshift boys they had been; they possessed, and they knew it, the clues to secrets more momentous than we could guess. They became slippery and difficult—but far from impossible. Shy, silent Jo scarcely counted now against the challenge of Rosie and Bet. Bet was brazen, Rosie provocative, and together they forced our paces. Bet was big for eleven and shabbily blonde, and her eyes were drowsy with insolence. 'Gis a wine-gum,' she'd say, ''an I'll show ya, if ya want.' (For a wine-gum she would have stripped in church.) Rosie, on the other hand, more devious and sly, had sharp salts of wickedness on her, and she led me a dance round the barns and fowls'-houses which often left me parched and trembling. What to do about either—Bet or Rosie—took a considerable time to discover.

Meanwhile, it was as though I had been dipped in hot oil, baked, dried and hung throbbing on wires. Mysterious senses clicked into play overnight, possessed one in luxuriant order, and one's body seemed tilted out of all recognition by shifts in its balance of power. It was the time when the thighs seemed to burn like dry grass, to cry for cool water and cucumbers, when the emotions swung drowsily between belly and hands, prickled, hungered, moulded the curves of the clouds; and when to lie face downwards in a summer field was to feel the earth's thrust go through you. Brother Jack and I grew suddenly more active, always running or shinning up trees, working ourselves into lathers of exhaustion, whereas till then we'd been inclined to indolence. It was not that we didn't know what was happening to us, we just didn't know what to do with it. And I might have been shinning up trees to this day if it hadn't been for Rosie Burdock. . . .

*   *   *

The day Rosie Burdock decided to take me in hand was a motionless day of summer,

286

creamy, hazy and amber-coloured, with the beech trees standing in heavy sunlight as though clogged with wild wet honey. It was the time of haymaking, so when we came out of school Jack and I went to the farm to help.

The whirr of the mower met us across the stubble, rabbits jumped like firecrackers about the fields, and the hay smelt crisp and sweet. The farmer's men were all hard at work, raking, turning and loading. Tall, whiskered fellows forked the grass, their chests like bramble patches. The air swung with their forks and the swathes took wing and rose like eagles to the tops of the wagons. The farmer gave us a short fork each and we both pitched in with the rest. . . .

I stumbled on Rosie behind a haycock, and she grinned up at me with the sly, glittering eyes of her mother. She wore her tartan frock and cheap brass necklace, and her bare legs were brown with hay-dust.

'Get out a there,' I said. 'Go on.'

Rosie had grown and was hefty now, and I was terrified of her. In her cat-like eyes and curling mouth I saw unnatural wisdoms more threatening than anything I could imagine. The last time we'd met I'd hit her with a cabbage stump. She bore me no grudge, just grinned.

'I got summat to show ya.'

'You push off,' I said.

I felt dry and dripping, icy hot. Her eyes glinted, and I stood rooted. Her face was wrapped in a pulsating haze and her body seemed to flicker with lightning.

'You thirsty?' she said.

'I ain't, so there.'

'You be,' she said. 'C'mon.'

So I stuck the fork into the ringing ground and followed her, like doom.

We went a long way, to the bottom of the field, where a wagon stood half-loaded. Festoons of untrimmed grass hung down like curtains all around it. We crawled underneath, between the wheels, into a herb-scented cave of darkness. Rosie scratched about, turned over a sack, and revealed a stone jar of cider.

'It's cider,' she said. 'You ain't to drink it though. Not much of it, any rate.'

Huge and squat, the jar lay on the grass like an unexploded bomb. We lifted it up, unscrewed the stopper, and smelt the whiff of fermented apples. I held the jar to my mouth and rolled my eyes sideways, like a beast at a waterhole. 'Go on,' said Rosie. I took a deep breath. . . .

Never to be forgotten, that first long secret drink of golden fire, juice of those valleys and of that time, wine of wild orchards, of russet summer, of plump red apples and Rosie's burning cheeks. Never to be forgotten, or ever tasted again. . . .

I put down the jar with a gulp and a gasp. Then I turned to look at Rosie. She was yellow and dusty with buttercups and seemed to be purring in the gloom; her hair was rich as a wild bee's nest and her eyes were full of stings. I did not know what to do about her, nor did I know what not to do. She looked smooth and precious, a thing of unplumbable mysteries, and perilous as quicksand.

'Rosie . . .' I said, on my knees, and shaking.

She crawled with a rustle of grass towards me, quick and superbly assured. Her hand in mine was like a small wet flame which I could neither hold nor throw away. Then Rosie, with a remorseless, reedy strength, pulled me down from my tottering perch, pulled me down, down into her wide green smile and into the deep subaqueous grass.

Then I remember little, and that little, vaguely. Skin drums beat in my head. Rosie was close-up, salty, an invisible touch, too near to be seen or measured. And it seemed that the wagon under which we lay went floating away like a barge, out over the valley

where we rocked unseen, swinging on motionless tides.

Then she took off her boots and stuffed
them with flowers. She did the same with
mine. Her parched voice crackled like flames
in my ears. More fires were started. I drank
more cider. Rosie told me outrageous fanta-
sies. She liked me, she said, better than Walt,
or Ken, Boney Harris or even the curate. And
I admitted to her, in a loud, rough voice, that
she was even prettier than Betty Gleed. For a
long time we sat with our mouths very close,
breathing the same hot air. We kissed, once
only, so dry and shy, it was like two leaves colliding in air.

At last the cuckoos stopped singing and slid
into the woods. The mowers went home and
left us. I heard Jack calling as he went down
the lane, calling my name till I heard him no
more. And still we lay in our wagon of grass
tugging at each other's hands, while her
husky, perilous whisper drugged me and the
cider beat gongs in my head. . . .

Night came at last, and we crawled out
from the wagon and stumbled together
towards home. Bright dew and glow-worms
shone over the grass, and the heat of the day
grew softer. I felt like a giant; I swung from
the trees and plunged my arms into nettles

just to show her. Whatever I did seemed valiant and easy. Rosie carried her boots, and smiled.

There was something about that evening which dilates the memory, even now. The long hills slavered like Chinese dragons, crimson in the setting sun. The shifting lane lassoed my feet and tried to trip me up. And the lake, as we passed it, rose hissing with waves and tried to drown us among its cannibal fish.

Perhaps I fell in—though I don't remember. But here I lost Rosie for good. I found myself wandering home alone, wet through, and possessed by miracles. I discovered extraordinary tricks of sight. I could make trees move and leap-frog each other, and turn bushes into roaring trains. I could lick up the stars like acid drops and fall flat on my face without pain. I felt magnificent, fateful, and for the first time in my life, invulnerable to the perils of night.

When at last I reached home, still dripping wet, I was bursting with power and pleasure. I sat on the chopping-block and sang 'Fierce Raged the Tempest' and several other hymns of that nature. I went on singing till long after supper-time, bawling alone in the dark. Then Harold and Jack came and frog-marched me to bed. I was never the same again. . . .

A year or so later occurred the Brith Wood rape. If it could be said to have occurred. By now I was one of a green-horned gang who went bellowing round the lanes, scuffling, fighting, aimless and dangerous, confused by our strength and boredom. Of course something like this was bound to happen, and it happened on a Sunday.

We planned the rape a week before, up in the builder's stable. The stable's thick air of mouldy chaff, dry leather and rotting straw, its acid floors and unwashed darkness provided the atmosphere we needed. We met there regularly to play cards and scratch and whistle and talk about girls.

There were about half a dozen of us that morning, including Walt Kerry, Bill Shepherd, Sixpence the Tanner, Boney and Clergy Green. The valley outside, seen through the open door, was crawling with April rain. We sat round on buckets sucking strips of harness. Then suddenly Bill Shepherd came out with it.

'Here,' he said. 'Listen. I got'n idea. . . .'

He dropped his voice into a furry whisper and drew us into a circle.

'You know that Lizzy Berkeley, don't ya?' he said. He was a fat-faced lad, powerful and shifty, with a perpetual caught-in-the-act look. 'She'd do,' he said. 'She's daft in the 'ead. She'd be all right, y'know.'

We thought about Lizzy and it was true enough; she was daft about religion. A short, plump girl of about sixteen, with large, blue-bottle eyes, she used to walk in Brith Wood with a handful of crayons writing texts on the trunks of the beech trees. Huge rainbow letters on the smooth green bark, saying 'JESUS LOVES ME NOW.'

'I seen 'er Sunday,' said Walt, 'an' she was at it then.'

'She's always at it,' said Boney.

'Jerusalem!' said Clergy in his pulpit voice.

'Well, 'ow about it?' said Bill.

We drew closer together, out of earshot of the horse. Bill rolled us in his round red eyes.

'It's like this, see. Blummin'-well simple.' We listened and held our breath. 'After church Sunday mornin' we nips up to the wood. An' when 'er comes back from chapel—we got 'er.'

We all breathed out. We saw it clearly. We saw her coming alone through the Sunday wood, chalk-coloured Lizzy, unsuspecting and holy, in the bundle of her clothes and

293

body. We saw her come walking through her text-chalked trees, blindly, straight into our hands.

'She'd 'oller,' said Boney.

'She's too batty,' said Bill.

'She'd think I was one of the 'possles.'

Clergy gave his whinnying, nervous giggle, and Boney rolled on the floor.

'You all on, then?' Bill whispered. 'Wha's say? 'Ow about it? It'll half be a stunt, you watch.'

We none of us answered, but we all felt committed; soon as planned, the act seemed done. We had seen it so vividly it could have happened already, and there was no more to be said. For the rest of the week we avoided each other, but we lived with our scruffy plan. We thought of little else but that coming encounter; of mad Lizzy and her stumpy, accessible body which we should all of us somehow know. . . .

On Sunday morning we trooped from the church and signalled to each other with our eyebrows. The morning was damp with a springtime sun. We nodded, winked, and jerked our heads, then made our separate ways to the wood. When we gathered at last at the point of ambush, the bounce had somehow gone out of us. We were tense and silent;

nobody spoke. We lay low as arranged, and waited.

We waited a long time. Birds sang, squirrels chattered, the sun shone; but nobody came. We began to cheer up and giggle.

'She ain't comin',' said someone. 'She seen Bill first.'

'She seen 'im and gone screamin' 'ome.'

"Er's lucky, then. I'd 'ave made 'er 'oller.'

'I'd 'ave run 'er up a tree.'

We were savage and happy, as though we'd won a battle. But we waited a little while longer.

'Sod it!' said Bill. 'Let's push off. Come on.' And we were all of us glad he'd said it.

At that moment we saw her, walking dumpily up the path, solemn in her silly straw hat. Bill and Boney went sickly pale and watched her in utter misery. She approached us slowly, a small fat doll, shafts of sunlight stroking her dress. None of us moved as she drew level with us, we just looked at Bill and Boney. They returned our looks with a kind of abject despair and slowly got to their feet.

What happened was clumsy, quick and meaningless; silent, like a very old film. The two boys went loping down the bank and barred the plump girl's way. She came to a halt and they all stared at each other. . . . The key moment of our fantasy; and trivial. After a gawky pause, Bill shuffled towards her and laid a hand on her shoulder. She hit him twice with her bag of crayons, stiffly, with the jerk of a puppet. Then she turned, fell down, got up, looked round, and trotted away through the trees.

Bill and Boney did nothing to stop her, they slumped and just watched her go. And the last we saw of our virgin Lizzy was a small round figure, like a rubber ball, bouncing down hill out of sight.

After that, we just melted away through the wood, separately, in opposite directions. I dawdled home slowly, whistling aimless tunes and throwing stones at stumps and gateposts. What had happened that morning was impossible to say. But we never spoke of it again.

As for our leaders, those red-fanged ravishers of innocence—what happened to them in the end? Boney was raped himself soon afterwards; and married his attacker, a rich farm-widow, who worked him to death in her bed and barnyard. Bill Shepherd met a girl who trapped him neatly by stealing his Post Office Savings Book. Walt went to sea and won prizes for cooking, then married into the fish-frying business. The others married too,

296

and raised large families, and became members of the Parish Church Council.

Of the little girls who had been our victims and educators, and who led us through those days: pretty Jo grew fat with a Painswick baker, lusty Bet went to breed in Australia, and Rosie, having baptized me with her cidrous kisses, married a soldier and I lost her for ever.

LAST DAYS

THE last days of my childhood were also the last days of the village. I belonged to that generation which saw, by chance, the end of a thousand years' life. The change came late to our Cotswold valley, didn't really show itself till the late 1920's; I was twelve by then, but during that handful of years I witnessed the whole thing happen.

Myself, my family, my generation, were born in a world of silence; a world of hard work and necessary patience, of backs bent to the ground, hands massaging the crops, of waiting on weather and growth; of villages like ships in the empty landscapes and the long walking distances between them; of white narrow roads, rutted by hooves and cart-wheels, innocent of oil or petrol, down which people passed rarely, and almost never for pleasure, and the horse was the fastest thing moving. Man and horse were all the power we had—abetted by levers and pulleys. But the horse was king, and almost everything grew around him: fodder, smithies, stables, paddocks, distances and the rhythm of our days. His eight miles an hour was the limit of our movements, as it had been since the days of the Romans. That eight miles an hour was life and death, the size of our world, our prison.

This was what we were born to, and all we knew at first. Then, to the scream of the horse, the change began. The brass-lamped motor-car came coughing up the road, followed by the clamorous charabanc; the solid-tyred bus climbed the dusty hills and more people came and went. Chickens and dogs were the early sacrifices, falling demented beneath the wheels. The old folk, too, had strokes and seizures, faced by speeds beyond comprehension. Then scarlet motor-bikes, the size of five-barred gates, began to appear in the village, on which our youths roared like rockets up the two-minute hills, then spent weeks making repairs and adjustments.

These appearances did not immediately alter our lives; the cars were freaks and rarely seen, the motor-bikes mostly in pieces, we used the charabancs only once a year, and our buses at first were experiments. Meanwhile Lew Ayres, wearing a bowler-hat, ran his wagonette to Stroud twice a week. The carriage held six, and the fare was twopence, but most people preferred to walk. Mr West, from Sheepscombe, ran a cart every day, and would carry your parcels for a penny. But most of us still did the journey on foot, heads down to the wet Welsh winds, ignoring the carters—whom we thought extortionate—and spending a long hard day at our shopping.

But the car-shying horses with their rolling eyes gave signs of the hysteria to come. Soon the village would break, dissolve and scatter, become no more than a place for pensioners. It had a few years left, the last of its thousand, and they passed almost without our knowing. They passed quickly, painlessly, in motor-bike jaunts, in the shadows of the new picture-palace, in quick trips to Gloucester (once a foreign city) to gape at the jazzy shops. Yet right to the end, like the false strength that precedes death, the old life seemed as lusty as ever.

The Church, for instance, had never appeared more powerful. Its confident bell rang out each Sunday; the village heard it, asked no questions, put on satin and serge, filed into the pews, bobbed and nodded, frowned at its children, crouched and prayed, bawled or quavered through hymns, and sat in blank rows or jerkily slept while the curate reeled off those literary sermons which he had hired from the ecclesiastical library.

Sunday, far from being a day of rest, was in some ways tougher than a weekday; it was never torpid and it gave one a lift, being a combination of both indulgence and discipline. On that one day in seven—having bathed the night before—we were clean, wore our best and ate meat. The discipline was Sunday School, learning the Collect, and worship both morning and evening. Neither mood nor inclination had any say in the matter, nor had doubt occurred to us yet.

Sunday mornings at home were the usual rush—chaos in the kitchen, shrill orders to wash, and everyone's eyes on the clock. We polished our hair with grease and water, and scrubbed ourselves under the pump. Being Sunday, there was a pound of large sausages for breakfast, fried black and bursting with fat. One dipped them in pepper and ate them in haste, an open prayer-book propped up by the plate.

'Heavens alive, you'll be late, our lad.'

Gobble, mumble and choke.

'What *are* you up to? Get a move on do.'

'Leave off—I'm learning the Collect.'

'What's that you say?'

'I-Gotta-Learn-Me-Collect!'

'Hurry up and learn it then.'

'I can't hurry up! Not if you keep on! . . .'

301

But it was really not difficult at all; ten inscrutable lines absorbed between mouthfuls, and usually on the run. Up the bank, down the road, the greasy prayer book in one hand, the remains of the sausage in the other: 'Almighty and Most Merciful Father, who alone worketh Great Marvels . . .' In five minutes it was all in my head.

At Sunday School Miss Bagnall, polishing her nose, said: 'The Collect—now who will oblige? . . .' I would jump to my feet and gabble, word perfect, the half page of sonorous syllables. It came in through the eyes and out through the mouth, and left no trace of its passing. Except that I can never read a Collect today without tasting a crisp burnt sausage. . . .

After an hour of Sunday School we all went to the church, the choir going straight to the vestry. Here we huddled ourselves into our grimy robes, which only got washed at Easter. The parson lined us up and gave us a short, sharp prayer; then we filed into the stalls, took our privileged places, and studied the congregation. The Sunday School infants packed the bleak north wing, heads fuzzy as frosted flowers. The rest of the church was black with adults, solemn in cat's-fur and feathers. Most were arranged in family groups, but here and there a young couple, newly engaged, sat red in the neck and hands. The leading benches contained our gentry, their pews marked with visiting cards: the Lords of the Manor, Squire Jones and the Croomes'; then the Army, the Carvossos and Dovetons; the rich and settled spinsters, the Misses Abels and Bagnalls; and finally the wealthier farmers. All were neatly arranged by protocol, with the Squire up front by the pulpit. Through prayers and psalms and rackety hymns he slept like a beaming child, save when a visiting preacher took some rhetorical flight when he'd wake with a loud, 'God damn!'

Morning service began with an organ voluntary, perhaps a Strauss waltz played very slow. The organ was old, and its creaks and sighs were often louder than the music itself. The organ was blown by an ordinary pump-handle which made the process equally rowdy; and Rex Brown, the blower, hidden away in his box—and only visible to us in the choir—enlivened the service by parodying it in mime or by carving girls' names on the woodwork.

But in the packed congregation solemnity ruled. There was power, lamentation, full-throated singing, heavy prayers and public

303

repentance. No one in the village stayed away without reason, and no one yet wished to do so. We had come to the church because it was Sunday, just as we washed our clothes on Monday. There was also God taking terrible notes—a kind of Squire-archical rent-collector, ever ready to record the tenants' back-sliding and to evict them if their dues weren't paid.

This morning service was also something else. It was a return to the Ark of all our species in the face of the ever-threatening flood. We are free of that need now and when the flood does come shall drown proud and alone, no doubt. As it was, the lion knelt down with the lamb, the dove perched on the neck of the hawk, sheep nuzzled wolf, we drew warmth from each other and knew ourselves beasts of one kingdom. . . .

That was Sunday morning. With the service over there was gossip among the gravestones, a slow walk home to roasted dinners, then a nap with *The News of the World*. The elders dozed sexily through the fat afternoon, while the young went again to Sunday School. Later came Evensong, which was as different from Matins as a tryst from a Trafalgar Square rally. The atmosphere was gentler, moonier, more private; the service was considered to be voluntary. We choir-boys, of course, were compelled to go, but for the rest they went who would.

The church at night, in the dark of the churchyard, was just a strip of red-fired windows. Inside, the oil-lamps and motionless candles narrowed the place with shadows. The display of the morning was absent now; the nave was intimate, and sleepy. Only a few solitary worshippers were present this time, each cloaked in a separate absorption: a Miss Bagnall, Widow White, the church-cleaning woman, a widower and the postman at the back. The service was almost a reverie, our hymns nocturnal and quiet, the psalms traditional and never varying so that one could sing them without a book. The scattered faithful, half-obscured by darkness, sang them as though to themselves. 'Lord, now lettest Thou Thy servant depart in peace . . .' It was sung, eyes closed, in trembling tones. It could not have been sung in the morning.

From the seats in the choir we watched the year turn: Christmas, Easter and Whitsun, Rogation Sunday and prayers for rain, the Church following the plough very close. Harvest Festival perhaps was the one we liked best, the one that came nearest home. Then

305

how heavily and abundantly was our small church loaded; the cream of the valley was used to decorate it. Everyone brought of his best from field and garden; and to enter the church on Harvest morning was like crawling head first into a horn of plenty, a bursting granary, a vegetable stall, a grotto of bright flowers. The normally bare walls sprouted leaves and fruits, the altar great stooks of wheat, and ornamental loaves as big as cartwheels stood parked by the communion rails. Bunches of grapes, from the Squire's own vines, hung blue from the lips of the pulpit. Gigantic and useless marrows abounded, leeks and onions festooned the pews, there were eggs and butter on the lectern shelves, the windows were heaped with apples, and the fat round pillars which divided the church were skirted with oats and barley.

Almost everyone in the congregation had some hand in these things. Square-rumped farmers and ploughmen in chokers, old gardeners and poultry keepers, they nodded and pointed and prodded each other to draw attention to what they had brought. The Church was older than its one foundation, was as old as man's life on earth. The seed of these fruits, and the seed of these men, still came from the same one bowl; confined to this valley and renewing itself here, it went back to the days of the Ice. Pride, placation and the continuity of growth were what we had come to praise. And even when we sang, 'All is safely gathered in,' knowing full well that some of Farmer Lusty's oats still lay rotting in the fields, the discrepancy didn't seem important.

I remember one particular Harvest Festival which perfectly summed up this feeling. I was not old enough then to be in the choir, and I was sitting beside Tony, who was three. It was his first Harvest Festival, but he'd heard much about it and his expectations were huge. The choir with banners, was fidgeting in the doorway, ready to start its procession. Tony gazed with glittering eyes around him, sniffing the juicy splendours. Then, in a moment of silence, just before the organ crashed into the hymn, he asked loudly, 'Is there going to be drums?'

It was a natural question, innocent and true. For neither drums, nor cymbals, nor trumpets of brass would have seemed out of place at that time.

*   *   *

The death of the Squire was not the death

of the church, though they drew to their end together. He died, and the Big House was sold by auction and became a Home for Invalids. The lake silted up, the swans flew away, and the great pike choked in the reeds. With the Squire's hand removed, we fell apart— though we were about to do so anyway. His servants dispersed and went into the factories. His nephew broke up the estate.

Fragmentation, free thought, and new excitements, came now to intrigue and perplex us. The first young couple to get married in a registry office were roundly denounced from the pulpit. 'They who play with fire shall be consumed by fire!' stormed the vicar. 'Ye mark my words!' Later he caught me reading *Sons and Lovers* and took it away and destroyed it. This may well have been one of his last authoritative gestures. A young apologist succeeded him soon.

Meanwhile the old people just dropped away—the white-whiskered, gaitered, booted and bonneted, ancient-tongued last of their world, who thee'd and thou'd both man and beast, called young girls 'damsels', young boys 'squires', old men 'masters', the Squire himself 'He', and who remembered the Birdlip stagecoach. Kicker Harris, the old coachman, with his top-hat and leggings, blew away like a torn-out page. Lottie Escourt, peasant shoot of a Norman lord, curled up in her relics and died. Others departed with hardly a sound. There was old Mrs Clissold, who sometimes called us for errands: 'Thee come up our court a minute, squire; I wants thee to do I a mission.' One ran to the shop to buy her a packet of bulls' eyes and was rewarded in the customary way. Bulls'-eye in cheek, she'd sink back in her chair and dismiss one with a sleepy nod. 'I ain't nurn a aypence about I just now—but Mrs Crissole'll recollect 'ee . . .' We wrote her off as the day's good deed, and she died still recollecting us.

★   ★   ★

Now the last days of my family, too, drew near, beginning with the courting of the girls.

I remember very clearly how it started. It was summer, and we boys were sitting on the bank watching a great cloud of smoke in the sky.

A man jumped off his bike and cried, 'It's the boiler-works!' and we ran up the hill to see it.

There was a fire at the boiler-works almost every year. When we got there we found it a

309

particularly good one. The warehouse, as usual, was sheathed in flame, ceilings and floors fell in, firemen shouted, windows melted like icicles, and from inside the building one heard thundering booms as the boilers started crashing about. We used up a lot of the day at this, cheering each toppling chimney.

When we got back to the village, much later in the evening, we saw a strange man down in our garden. We studied him from a distance with some feeling of shock. No one but neighbours and visiting relations had ever walked there before. Yet this ominous stranger was not only wandering free, he was being accompanied by all our women.

We rushed down the bank and burst roughly upon them, to find everyone crack-jawed with politeness. Our sisters cried La! when they saw us coming, and made us welcome as though we'd been round the world. Marjorie was particularly soft and loving, the others beamed anxiously at us; Mother, though not smart, was in her best black dress, and the stranger was twisting his hat.

'These are our brothers,' said Marjorie, grabbing two of us close to her bosom. 'This is Jackie and Loll, and that one's Tone. They're all of them terrible bad.'

There was nervous laughter and relief at this, as though several dark ghosts had been laid. We smirked and wriggled, aped and showed off, but couldn't think what was going on. In fact, the day of that boiler-works fire marked a beacon in the life of our girls. It was the day when their first young man came courting, and this stranger was he, and he was Marjorie's, and he opened a path through the garden.

He was handsome, curly-haired, a builder of barges, very strong, and entirely acceptable. His name was Maurice, and we boys soon approved him and gave him the run of the place. He was followed quite quickly by two other young men, one each for Dorothy and Phyllis. Dorothy got Leslie, who was a shy local scoutmaster, at least until he met her; Phyllis in turn produced Harold the bootmaker, who had fine Latin looks, played the piano by ear, and sang songs about old-fashioned mothers. Then Harold, our brother, got the infection too, mended our chairs, re-upholstered the furniture, and brought home a girl for himself.

At these strokes our home life changed forever; new manners and notions crept in; instead of eight in the kitchen there were now a round dozen, and so it stayed till the girls started marrying. The young men called nightly, with candles in jars, falling headlong down our precipitous bank; or came pushing their bikes on summer evenings loitering with the girls in the lanes; or sat round the fire talking slowly of work; or sat silent, just being there; while the sewing-machine hummed, and Mother rambled, and warm ripples of nothing lapped round them. They were wary of Mother, unsure of her temper, though her outbursts were at the world, not people. Leslie was tactful and diffident, giving short sharp laughs at her jokes. Maurice often lectured her on 'The Working Man Today', which robbed her of all understanding. Phyl's Harold would sometimes draw up to the piano, strike the keys with the strength of ten, then charm us all by bawling 'Because' or 'An Old Lady Passing By'.

Then there was cheese and cocoa, and 'Goodnight all', and the first one got up to leave. There followed long farewells by the back-kitchen door, each couple taking their turn. Those waiting inside had to bide their time. 'Our Doth! Ain't you finished yet?' 'Shan't be a minute.' Yum-yum, kiss-kiss. 'Well, hurry up do! You're awful.' Five more minutes of silence outside, then Marge shakes the latch on the door. 'How much longer, our

Doth? You been there all night. There's some got to work tomorrow,' 'All right, don't get ratty. He's just off now. Night-night, my beautiful bab.' One by one they departed; we turned down the lights, and the girls heaved themselves to bed.

Sundays, or Bank Holidays, were day-long courtships, and then the lovers were all over us. When it rained it was hopeless and we just played cards, or the boy friends modelled for dress-making. When fine perhaps Mother would plan a small treat, like a picnic in the woods.

I remember a sweltering August Sunday. Mother said it would be nice to go out. We would walk a short mile to a nice green spot and boil a kettle under the trees. It sounded simple enough, but we knew better. For Mother's picnics were planned on a tribal scale, with huge preparations beforehand. She flew round the kitchen issuing orders and the young men stood appalled at the work. There were sliced cucumbers and pots of paste, radishes, pepper and salt, cakes and buns and macaroons, soup-plates of bread and butter, jam, treacle, jugs of milk, and several fresh-made jellies.

The young men didn't approve of this at all, and muttered it was blooming mad. But

313

with a 'You carry that now, there's a dear boy,' each of us carried something. So we set off at last like a frieze of Greeks bearing gifts to some woodland god—Mother, with a tea-cloth over her head, gathering flowers as she went along, the sisters following with cakes and bread, Jack with the kettle, Tony with the salt, myself with a jug of milk; then the scowling youths in their blue serge suits carrying the jellies in open basins—jellies which rapidly melted in the sun and splashed them with yellow and rose. The young men swapped curses under their breath, brother Harold hung back in shame, while Mother led the way with prattling songs determined to make the thing go.

She knew soon enough when people turned sour and moved mountains to charm them out of it, and showed that she knew by a desperate gaiety and by noisy attacks on silence.

Now come along, Maurice, best foot forward, mind how you go, tee-hee. Leslie! just look at those pretty what-d'you-call'ems—those what's-its—*aren't* they a picture? I said Leslie, look, aren't they pretty, my dear? Funny you don't know the name. Oh, isn't it a scrumptious day, tra-la? Boys, isn't it a scrumptious day?'

Wordy, flustered, but undefeated, she got

us to the woods at last. We were ordered to scatter and gather sticks and to build a fire for the kettle. The fire smoked glumly and stung our eyes, the young men sat round like martyrs, the milk turned sour, the butter fried on the bread, cake crumbs got stuck to the cucumber, wasps seized the treacle, the kettle wouldn't boil and we ended by drinking the jellies.

As we boys would eat anything, anywhere, none of this bothered us much. But the young courting men sat on their spread silk-handkerchiefs and gazed at the meal in horror. 'No thanks, Mrs Lee. I don't think I could. I've just had me dinner, ta.'

They were none of them used to such disorder, didn't care much for open-air picnics—but most of all they were wishing to be away with their girls, away in some field or gulley, where summer and love would be food enough, and an absence of us entirely.

*   *   *

When the girls got engaged heavy blushes followed as the rings were shown to the family. 'It's a cluster of brilliants. Cost more than two pounds. He got it at Gloucester Market.' Now that things were official, there

315

was more sitting in the dark and a visible increase in tensions. The girls were now grown and they wished to be gone. They were in love and had found their men. Meanwhile, impatience nagged at them all, till in one case it suddenly exploded. . . .

It was evening. I was drawing at the kitchen table. One of the girls was late. When she came at last we had finished supper. She arrived with her boy, which seemed unusual, as it wasn't his calling-night.

'Well, take your coat off,' said Mother. 'Sit down.'

'No, thank you,' he answered frozenly.

'Don't just stand there—stiff as stiff can be.'

'I'm all right, Mrs Lee, I assure you.'

'Ma, we've been thinking—' the sister began. Her voice was level and loud.

I always went still at the sound of trouble, and didn't turn round or look. I just worked at my drawing, and each line and detail became inscribed with the growing argument. A pencilled leaf, the crook of a branch, each carried a clinging phrase: 'Don't talk so daft. . . . You're acting very funny. . . . You don't none of you know what I feel. . . . It's cruel to hear you talk like that. . . . I never had a proper chance. . . . Oh, come and sit down and don't act so silly. . . . It's no good, we made up our minds. . . . She's just about had enough, Mrs Lee, it's time she was out of it all. . . .' My pencil paused; what did they mean?

The other girls were indignant, Mother sad and lost, the argument rose and fell. 'Well, that's what *we* think, anyway. It's a scandal, you coming like this. What about him?—he just walks in—who does he think he is? What about *you*, if it comes to that? Well, what about us? we're listening. You think the whole place is just run for you. We don't! You do! We never! Well, come on girl, I've had enough!' Shocked pause, aghast. 'You dare!'

I was listening with every nerve and muscle of my back. Nothing happened; words flared and died. At last we boys went up to bed, undressed and lay in the dark. As we lay, still listening, the kitchen grew quieter, the trouble seemed to fade to a murmur. . . . Suddenly, there was uproar, the girls screaming, Mother howling, and a scuffling and crashing of furniture. Jack and I sprang instantly from our beds and tore downstairs in our shirts. We found Mother and two sisters at the young man's throat, bouncing him against the wall. The other girl was trying to pull them away. The whole was a scene of chaos. Without hesitation, and in spite of the congestion, we

317

sprang at the young man too.

But by the time we reached him the battle was over, the women had broken off. The young man stood panting, alone in the corner. I gave him a shove, he gave me a swipe, then he bent down to look for his hat.

He had tried to carry off our willing sister and we had all of us very near killed him. Now, just as suddenly, everybody was kissing each other, weeping, embracing, forgiving. Mother put her arm round the young man's neck and nearly strangled him afresh with affection. The whole party moved out into the dark back-kitchen, sniffing, and murmuring; 'There, there. It's all right. We're all friends now, aren't we? Dear boy. . . . Oh, Mother . . . There, there . . .'

A moment before I'd been blind with anger, ready to slay for the family. Now the rage was over, cancelled, let down. I turned in disgust from their billing and cooing; went up to the fire, lifted my nightshirt, and warmed my bare loins on the fire-guard. . . .

*　　　*　　　*

The girls were to marry; the Squire was dead; buses ran and the towns were nearer. We began to shrug off the valley and look

318

more to the world, where pleasures were more anonymous and tasty. They were coming fast, and we were nearly ready for them. Each week Miss Bagnall held her penny dances where girls' shapes grew more familiar. For a penny one could swing them through Lancers and Two-Steps across the resinous floor of the Hut—but if one swung them entirely off their feet then Miss B locked the piano and went home. . . .

Time squared itself, and the village shrank, and distances crept nearer. The sun and moon, which once rose from our hill, rose from London now in the East. One's body was no longer a punching ball, to be thrown against trees and banks, but a telescoping totem crying strange demands few of which we could yet supply. In the faces of the villagers one could see one's change, and in their habits their own change also. The horses had died; few people kept pigs any more but spent their spare time buried in engines. The flutes and cornets, the gramophones with horns, the wind harps were thrown away—now wireless aerials searched the electric sky for the music of the Savoy Orpheans. Old men in the pubs sang, 'As I Walked Out', then walked out and never came back. Our Mother was grey now, and a shade more lightheaded, talking of mansions she would never build.

As for me—for me, the grass grew longer, and more sorrowful, and the trees were surfaced like flesh, and girls were no more to be treated lightly but were creatures of commanding sadness, and all journeys through the valley were now made alone, with passion in every bush, and the motions of wind and cloud and stars were suddenly for myself alone, and voices elected me of all men living and called me to deliver the world, and I groaned from solitude, blushed when I stumbled, loved strangers and bread and butter, and made long trips through the rain on my bicycle, stared wretchedly through lighted windows, grinned wryly to think how little I was known, and lived in a state of raging excitement.

The sisters, as I said, were about to get married. Harold was working at a factory lathe. Brother Jack was at Grammar School, and his grammar was excellent; and Tony still had a fine treble voice. My Mother half-knew me, but could not help, I felt doomed, and of all things wonderful.

It was then that I began to sit on my bed and stare out at the nibbling squirrels, and to make up poems from intense abstraction, hour after unmarked hour, imagination

scarcely faltering once, rhythm hardly
skipping a beat, while sisters called me, suns
rose and fell, and the poems I made, which I
never remembered, were the the first and last
of that time. . . .

ST